DIRLANDAS

Telephones:
01-607 1874
01-609 4298

KEBAB HOUSE
GREEK TAVERN
FULLY LICENCED

Proprietor: MARIOS

2-3, North View Parade,
Tufnell Park Rd.,
London, N.7.
(Opposite ODEON Cinema)
OFF HOLLOWAY RD

TAVERNA

To Bapou Eftihi and Bapou Taki. For coming
to England, working hard and shouting about
our heritage. And to Yiayia Maroulla and
Yiayia Martha. For being the inspiring matriarchs,
driving forces, and cooks behind it all.

**GEORGINA
HAYDEN**

Taverna

Recipes from a Cypriot Kitchen

■ SQUARE PEG

Contents

Introduction

I have collected the recipes and dreamt about this book for as long as I can remember.

—

When I was young I would help both my yiayias in the kitchen, absorbing every bit of information I could and hoping their cooking sensibilities would rub off on to me. Shelling broad beans, filling bourekia (sweet ricotta and cinnamon filled pastries), and rolling out hundreds of cheesy flaounes for what felt like the entire Cypriot community are just some of the many food memories of my childhood.

Both my grandparents moved to England in the 1950s. My dad's parents opened and ran a successful Cypriot taverna in Tufnell Park for almost 30 years: it was the heart of our family and the inspiration behind the title of this book. We all lived in the flats upstairs – my grandparents and aunt included – and even when my parents, sister Lulu and I moved out we would still spend our weekends there. After Saturday Greek school (my most hated of all days), Lulu and I would run straight to the restaurant and try and help our yiayia set up by laying tables, filling the salt and pepper pots and cleaning. In reality we mostly got under her feet and would be sent upstairs to play instead, or to the back yard. The kitchen was small by restaurant standards today, but big enough for my grandparents to cook everything from scratch. It was a galley style kitchen, with an enormous grill for all the kebabs and meat. My yiayia would work all day making the dips, preparing all the mezedes, slow-cooking stews, stuffing vine leaves and baking trays of sweets. My bapou was obsessive about cleanliness and every piece of crockery, cutlery and glassware was wiped to within an inch of its life. It was a true Mediterranean kitchen – vocal, fiery and passionate – and everyone wanted to be a part of it. Every holiday or celebration was spent there – it was a huge space and big enough for all arms of our sprawling family to be together. New Year's Eve was my favourite of these days, as the restaurant would be open for business and heaving with regulars. Us grandkids would be ushered upstairs and kept there until around 11p.m. We would play games and dress up, and then when all the customers had finished their meals we were allowed back downstairs to party. Being small often meant falling asleep under a table or on a chair shortly after midnight, but boy it was worth it.

My mum's parents, equally food driven, opened one of the first Cypriot grocers and delis in North London and imported all our traditional ingredients.

Customers would come from miles away to shop there. It is hard to imagine now, but items such as halloumi, dried beans, lentils, even olive oil were not commonly found in supermarkets in the 1960s like they are today. They were a formidable pair, whom I miss dearly. My bapou worked insanely hard, starting out with nothing and working all the hours God sent in a Wall's sausage factory before opening his first shop. They retired before I was born but I have always enjoyed the stories. The first thing my aunt and my mum mention when talking about the grocer's was the smell, how evocative it was. All the produce was in sacks, large barrels, nothing was pre-packaged. Sacks of louvi, fasoles (black-eyed peas and white beans), strings of loukanika and mounds of seasonal fruit, veg and herbs. Huge tubs of different olives, including a special olive from their home village of Lythrodontas, which is famous for its groves. A huge wheel of kefalotyri that would stay out all day and be sold by the slice. Halloumi in brine, boxes of salt cod, fresh bread delivered every day and shelves of baklava, galato-boureko and kataifi. My mum would stand on stacked boxes of Coca Cola cans to reach the scales and weigh up pound bags of all the dry ingredients.

Every Sunday the shop would be shut and my mum would go with my bapou and help clear it out. She was small enough to get into the fridges and climb in and clean them. Once home he would take a long bath, filled with Radox, then drive his much prized Mercedes to Leicester Square for his weekly coffee-shop visit. My yiayia never knew what to expect in the afternoons, as he would often bring back homeless people he had met while out on his errands or drives. His big heart, and poor upbringing, made him empathetic and he would take in anyone he met and bonded with and would feed them. The house was always filled with people and food. Even when we were young, and my grandparents had retired, they still loved visiting Leicester Square and would take us for Chinese coconut buns on Gerrard Street, one of my favourite childhood memories.

Feasting, family and community is not just the bedrock of my family, but of Cypriot culture. Growing up it was so ingrained in our everyday life I almost took it for granted, not fully appreciating that this wasn't everybody's reality. As an adult I've realised how much this has influenced how I cook. Food is the soundtrack to my family life. Not just for big family events like birthday parties or religious holidays, but also food that captures quieter moods and moments of connection. Like my first book, *Stirring Slowly*, the recipes in this book reflect all those different moments of life: from meat feasts and mezedes to pared-back vegan weeknight dinners.

Cypriot food has all these bases covered. It is steeped in tradition and rituals. There are foods that heal, like the avgolemoni on page 161 and foods that celebrate, like the flaounes on page 260. There are also all the incredible influences. With its Greek and Turkish heritage, English rule and Middle Eastern neighbours, Cyprus is a melting point of ingredients, flavours and recipes. On the one hand there are quintessentially Greek aspects like eating a village salad with the sweetest tomatoes and creamiest feta, while looking out on to turquoise sea. On the other hand there is the use of cumin and coriander in our cooking, which are undoubtedly Eastern influences.

One of the first things people ask me when I explain that I am from Cyprus is 'Greek or Turkish?' Although I am Greek Cypriot, this book is completely personal and not political. If anything I am Cypriot first and foremost. Take the iconic recipe: stuffed vine leaves. In Greece they are called 'dolmathes', in Turkey they are called 'dolma', in Cyprus they are called 'koupepia' (or as we actually say it, 'koubebia' – Cypriots pronounce 'pi' softer than mainland Greeks) and so that's what I call them in this book. Stuffing vine leaves and other veg is an ancient tradition right across Eastern Europe and the Middle East. And my recipe doesn't claim to be definitive – these are the recipes I have grown up with. The ones passed down to me from my yiayias, my mum, my aunts, and that I want to pass down also.

At the same time I live a modern life with my own tastes, time pressures and shopping landscape. This book is my take on traditional recipes, some of them straight from my yiayia, others tweaked to make them more accessible and the ingredients more obtainable. Much as I would love to give you my Yiayia Martha's exact recipe for (her addictive) taramosalata, it is near impossible. Hardly anyone would be able to find the roe she uses so I have adapted it so it is as close as can be.

Taverna is a book of memories, appreciation and family. I've written the intro for this book a thousand times in my heart, and it has been near impossible. Where do I begin? There are so many memories. You'll find countless stories in the intros to the recipes. Almost all of them have a history. I so badly want you to love this as much as I do, and that is the hard part. A lot of this book is laced with nostalgia and emotion; however, I feel confident enough to say that even without the strong memories you will hopefully find a place in your heart and home for the recipes also.

An introduction to Cypriot food

—

Having one of the strongest orthodox churches in the world means that many religious Greeks and Cypriots spend much of their time fasting and eating restrictive diets – these Lenten days make up around a third of the year. For weeks leading up to Easter and Christmas a mostly vegan diet is adopted. Recipes were created to accommodate these days, using items such as tahini and honey to make Lenten sweets, and plenty of pulses and fresh veg to create hearty stews. You'll find that many homes, particularly those inland, still grow and cultivate their own crops and press their own olive oil, leading self-sufficient seasonal lifestyles.

On the opposite end of the spectrum are the festivals and religious holidays. Saint days are a big deal, with associated villages and churches holding a 'panayiri', a church fête open to everyone. You'll find stalls, games, rides and, most importantly, copious numbers of street food vendors. Industrial-sized barbecues are set up, and loukoumades (moreish little deep-fried dough balls drenched in rose and clove syrup, see page 227) are made en masse.

The most important time of year, however, is Easter, during which weeks of baking take place in preparation for the big weekend. Easter fast is broken straight after Midnight Mass on the Saturday, when families run home and devour bowls of magiritsa, a rich, creamy lamb offal soup. The lamb which the offal comes from is then slowly barbecued whole on Easter day. The Sunday is an entire village affair and in my opinion the best day of the year in rural Cyprus and Greece.

One of my favourite Easter Sundays took place in Phini, my grandpa's village in the Troodos mountains. It meant a 7a.m. church service directly followed by glasses of wine, bread – and shots of ouzo for the brave. Families went home to eat and then the village began to congregate in the local schoolyard for games and races. Meanwhile a feast was being prepared in the local square, with whole lambs on spits being basted in red wine and oregano for several hours. The roads were closed, the streets were lined with tables and chairs and a feast was had. There were potatoes, endless salads, pita, dips, wine and an abundance of the tender fragrant lamb. After dinner coffee was made, the bottles of ouzo and zinvania returned (from the church service in the morning) and a band appeared. We stayed until the early hours, drinking and dancing, then danced down the cobbled streets home, full and happy.

And what about between the extremes, when we aren't fasting, there isn't a celebration or a banquet being held? Our everyday food is still never just a meal, it is always an array of dishes. Eating at friends' houses growing up it surprised me when I was presented with a plate of food. Food was and is never plated and served to us at home, it was always brought to the table and served in situ with many, many accompaniments. As well as the main meal, whatever that may be, the bare minimum would be a salad (even with hot food), bread (to not have bread is unthinkable), a plate of lemons and chillies, olives, a tub of Cypriot yoghurt (tangier than Greek yoghurt) and always a bottle of 'kalo lathi' – good extra virgin olive oil, for dressing. Then, depending on the food, you might also have pickled caper stalks, beetroot, and something cooked in eggs would also make an appearance (see pages 31 and 107). All this would accompany even a saucepan of simply cooked lentils. A meal is never just a meal, it is always a mini meze.

HINTS, TIPS AND SHOPPING

You don't need any specific cooking skills when preparing Greek and Cypriot food, there are no unusual cooking methods, but a few shopping and prepping hints and tips may make your life easier, and quicker.

With every trip to Cyprus and Greece I have discovered something new: the old carob mill not too far from the family home in Limassol, tea made with cherry stalks in the Troodos mountains, and pickling caper stalks (thorns and all) in the spring. And on top of that there are hints, tips and tricks passed down, from how to peel tomatoes in no time at all (a much-needed skill for a lot of recipes) to Mama Socratous' fail-safe way of making the creamiest avgolemoni, with not a scrambled egg in sight.

FRUIT AND VEG
As with all cuisines and recipes, try to cook seasonally, using the best ingredients available to you. For me there is nothing quite like the excitement during August when I know there is a specific type of marrow and fresh black-eyed beans to cook. As a family we eat this every Saturday until the season is over, and when it has finished we look forward to eating

it again the following year. Why ruin a beautiful, simple and delicious dish by using bland, tasteless, out of season ingredients? During the summer you will find strawberry carts all over Cyprus, selling literally nothing but the sweetest plumpest strawberries. No one would dream of buying or selling them any other time of year. This applies to most of the produce we buy: juicy ripe tomatoes in the warmer months, pounds of citrus when the temperature drops (although you will almost always find lemons on trees, even if the fruit is green). Visit your greengrocer or local market and ask them what is around at the moment, then plan your recipes accordingly. If there is an unusual ingredient you want to try but can't find, just ask: many grocers can source them for you, they just may not stock them all the time.

And on a very specific vegetable note, biased as I am, there really is nothing quite like a Cyprus potato. Because of the Cypriot soil these beauties are golden in colour, waxy and are phenomenal when roasted. They're naturally incredibly buttery, and not as hard to find as you might think, so be sure to seek them out.

STORING AND PREPARING FRUIT AND VEG

Potatoes, artichokes and apples: Half fill a large bowl with cold water and add a lemon, halved. Pop the prepped veg into the water while you are peeling and they won't discolour. You can also do this ahead of time, if need be, leaving them in the water for a couple of hours before use.

Tomatoes: Peeling tomatoes is an important part of Greek cooking. Peel them easily by cutting a small cross, only 1–2cm each way, at the top of each tomato and place in a large heatproof bowl. Cover the tomatoes with boiling water and leave for a minute or two. Drain from the water and you will be able to easily peel away the skins, using the cut as a starting point. The other way is to grate the tomatoes. This is a little messier, but if you have a coarse handheld grater it should be easy. By grating a ripe tomato, you naturally separate the flesh and seeds from the skin, which you just discard. Both methods work in my recipes.

Prickly pears: Having always had these beautiful, funny little fruits pre-pared for me by my grandmother, I never fully appreciated their aggressive exterior, until one day when I was caught out at our local grocer's. A friend and I, holidaying in Cyprus, went to the local shop, and in an attempt to impress with my knowledge of all the unusual produce I grabbed a handful of these little beauties. They had not, however, been prepared yet and were still covered with their little thorns. The staff gasped, and I squealed in pain. Hundreds of little thorns covered the palms of my hands! The only way to remove them is with a ton of olive oil and a knife. My advice? Buy them ready cleaned. Alternatively stick a fork into the top of the fruit, hold it over a rubbish bowl and cut the outer skin off. Or get a yiayia to do it for you.

Mespila: Small orange-coloured oblong fruits that look like less fuzzy apricots, more commonly known as loquats or nespole. They're sweet but also have a slight tartness to them. The best time to eat a loquat is when the skin starts to turn brown and looks almost bruised (we would always peel the skin). Delicious roasted with honey and almonds, and served alongside ice cream, or even panna cotta (this was our wedding pudding).

Aubergines and cucumbers: You will often notice that aubergines and cucumbers in Greek cooking have had their skins partially removed, in a stripy fashion. The only reason I have found for this is that many people find the skins hard to digest, particularly aubergine. It is a habit I have picked up from my grandma and one I still follow today; for whatever reason, I do prefer my aubergine skin in stripes.

Fresh black-eyed beans or peas: Not something commonly found in the UK; however, if you live near a good Greek grocer's you might be lucky enough to come across them in the summer months. They look like slightly thicker, longer green beans and are filled with tender fresh little black-eyed peas. Remove the string/thread and cook young beans in plenty of water until tender. Larger beans can be split, and you can cook just the peas. Cook and serve simply finished with lots of lemon, salt and extra virgin olive oil.

Vine leaves: Unless you live near a Greek, Turkish or Middle Eastern grocer's, vine leaves might be hard to purchase. But you have two options – buy them in brine, which you can do in larger supermarkets and online. Just be sure to blanch or soak them first to remove the excess salt. Or grow your own, which is really simple. We always have bags of fresh vine leaves in the freezer after raiding friends' vines, stocking up for the colder months.

Horta/wild greens: Horta is probably the Greek word I get asked about the most. What are horta and where can we find them? Horta is an all-round term for wild greens, weeds even, plants found on the side of roads, up

mountains. It isn't a single type of plant – it can be dandelion, amaranth, roka (wild rocket), nettles, hartwort, mustard greens . . . the list goes on. In reality most people won't be able to find a lot of these greens, but do not be disheartened, any recipe calling for horta can often be substituted with more accessible greens such as spinach and chard.

Salad: Buy your salad in bunches and whole heads of lettuce rather than bags of picked leaves. They will last longer – just wash them well and store them in a cloth-lined drawer in your fridge; much more flavoursome and far cheaper.

Herbs: For convenience, supermarket herbs are fine, but they are often overpriced and not always as flavourful as they could be. There is nothing quite like the coriander my mum buys from the local Greek grocer – it is far more aromatic and less than half the price. Seek out local international grocers and markets for more flavoursome options. Also, if you find you have an abundance of herbs, try chopping them up and freezing them. This saves on waste and means you always have them to hand. My yiayia would always give us bags of chopped parsley to have in the freezer, just in case.

MEAT AND FISH

Meat: After many years as a vegetarian, I started eating meat again in my early 20s. As a result I have a diet that is rich in vegetables and pulses, with meat or fish occasionally thrown in. I don't rely on meat as a main ingredient in my cooking, and can happily eat for days without it. I buy the best I can afford, and always make sure it is British and, where appropriate, higher welfare. I appreciate not everyone has these options or choices, it is just the way I like to cook.

Cheaper cuts of meat: Keep an eye out for special offers on things like lamb shoulder, shanks, pork shoulder, chicken thighs. Essentially anything which requires slow cooking, as a lot of our meat dishes do, will freeze perfectly well for a few months.

Fish: The same principle applies to fish; try to buy fish with an MSC logo, as you can be assured it has been responsibly sourced, and if in doubt ask your fishmonger, as they'll be up to date with which fish are endangered and which are in abundance. The list is ever-changing, so it is always good to ask.

How to prepare shellfish: Shellfish can be intimidating but I promise it isn't too difficult. The key thing to remember when cooking mussels and clams, for example, is that before cooking they should be tightly shut (alive) and not chipped, and when they have been cooked they need to have opened. If they are open before cooking, tap where the two shells meet lightly (with the side of a butter knife) and the shell should shut. If it doesn't, it is dead – throw it away. Equally, once cooked if any haven't opened, chuck them, they aren't good for eating.

DAIRY

Most Greek and Cypriot cheeses can be found easily, with halloumi being a household staple for many non-Cypriots. Where possible I have given options and alternatives.

Anari: This is one of our most popular cheeses, and very similar to Italian ricotta. Fresh anari is a little denser, less wet, so if you are substituting with ricotta make sure you strain off any liquid in the tub. And salted anari is very similar to Italian salted ricotta, which is a little more accessible.

Kefalotyri: A salty hard white cheese which can be used in a variety of ways – fried for dishes like saganaki, or grated over pasta or salads. If you can't find it, a firm pecorino is a good substitute.

Flaouna cheese: A mild cheese that is made especially to make flaounes. You'll find it mostly in the lead up to Orthodox Easter, and just after.

Cypriot yoghurt: I've listed Greek yoghurt in the recipes but if you *can* find Cypriot yoghurt then give it a try. It is set but slightly tangier than Greek. Perfect with savoury foods.

DRY INGREDIENTS

If you live in a big city, the chances are you will be blessed with international shops and markets. If you don't, then chances are that most of the large supermarkets will stock what you need. You can usually find slightly more unusual ingredients in a special section of the store, with those such as tahini and rose water becoming more commonplace. At the back of the book, however, I have listed a few Greek specialist shops and websites that are great if you are stuck.

Cooking chickpeas: Place the chickpeas in a large bowl and cover with plenty of cold water. Stir in a couple of teaspoons of bicarbonate of soda and cover loosely with cling film. Leave to soak for 24 hours. When they're ready, drain and rinse them well and place in a large saucepan. Cover with cold water and place on a high heat. Bring to the boil, then reduce to a simmer. Cook for around an hour, then check. They should be buttery and soft – if they're not quite there, keep going. Depending how old they are, they can take a few hours – but be sure to keep the hot water topped up. When they're tender, remove from the heat and leave to cool completely in the cooking liquor so they swell up.

Beans: Always soak overnight, otherwise they will take forever to cook or soften and your dish will be ruined. Do this and you will be rewarded with tender creamy pulses.

Village flour and niseste: Village flour is typical of Cyprus and you will always find a bag in every Greek yiayia's kitchen. It is a type of durum flour that is used for making pasta, like the ravioles on page 112. Niseste is a typical Greek cornflour that is used in creams, puddings and sauces.

Rose water and orange blossom water: These perfumed waters may not be to everyone's palate, however I do think that is mostly because they are misused and added with a heavy hand. If using, remember to use sparingly – you don't want to feel like you have consumed a bottle of perfume. Similarly add them to dishes after cooking, as their flavour and scent can be lost when heated. Flavour cakes and sweets by adding them to syrups and creams.

Carob: For hundreds of years carob has been one of Cyprus's biggest exports, and was nicknamed the 'black gold of Cyprus'. The pods look like large, flat vanilla pods, and you can buy the syrup relatively easily now. Using it adds a natural sweetness and depth, likened to chocolate. Wonderful in baking.

Tahini: Thankfully tahini is so popular now that you can find it in most supermarkets. It is a sesame paste, not too dissimilar to peanut butter in texture. A key ingredient in both sweet and savoury Cypriot dishes.

Commandaria: A sweet dessert wine made in the foothills of the Troodos mountains. Beautiful, and is the world's oldest named wine still in production. If you like port or a sweet sherry, you'll love it (if you can't find it for the recipes, use one of these instead). It is also what is used for communion in Greek Cypriot churches, meaning we all get a taste for it from a young age.

Mastiha/mastic: A very popular flavouring and ingredient in Greek cooking, mastic is resin collected from the mastic tree, traditionally from the island of Chios. You can buy small jars of it, and it comes in its resin form. To cook with it, it must be ground first, with a little sugar to stop it sticking to the mortar. Don't be tempted by pre-ground mastic, as it will have less flavour.

Mehlepi: Another popular flavouring (often used in conjunction with mastic in Cypriot cooking), mehlepi is the stone from the kernel of the St Lucie cherry. Again, it must be ground before using, and don't use too much or it'll make the food bitter.

Glyko/spoon sweets: You won't find a single home in Cyprus where there isn't at least one jar of glyko (spoon sweets) lurking somewhere. It is a popular way of preserving fruit, and even some vegetables. Expect to find jars of candied 'kitromilo' – bitter orange rind, wet walnuts, even baby aubergines, glacé-like and stored in their syrup. Always served on a small plate, with a mini fork and a glass of ice-cold water.

Extra virgin olive oil: Or as we say 'kalo lathi' – good oil. Be sure to invest in the best quality extra virgin olive oil you can afford. Don't use your good oil for cooking, it's a waste, but be sure to dress salads, mezedes and stews with a drizzle or two for a beautiful finish. And if you want to be super savvy, buy a large drum of oil from any good Greek grocer's: you'll get more liquid gold for your buck.

1

BREAKFAST

—

A CYPRIOT INSPIRED BREAKFAST, ANY TIME OF THE DAY

Breakfast growing up was a bit of a confusing meal. The adults would start the day with a sugar-laden coffee and 1–4 cigarettes (which I think could be said of a lot of older-generation Greeks), and we would start the day with a glass of milk and slices of cake – very Mediterranean. However, in the evening we would often have the equivalent of 'breakfast' but for dinner, which was truly one of my favourite meals. It was a combination of meze and breakfast and was just a complete feast and felt hugely indulgent. As you can see, it's not so much a recipe, but a guide, a recommendation of which dishes could be served together to create the perfect start to the day. People love being presented with many plates of small things, and the same can be said for breakfast; it's impressive and feels like such a treat. Also, it may look like a lot of work, but most of it can be made ahead. (And if you do fancy trying your hand at my favourite breakfast cake of choice, check out page 45 for my chocolate and halva marble cake.)

OLIVES AND PICKLES

A small selection of olives is a necessity at the breakfast table. Or at any Greek table. Whatever the time of day. And the same goes for pickles: we'll always have a selection of whatever is going to accompany a meal – whether that's whole green peppers, caper leaves or beetroot.

HOUMOUS (PAGE 57)

Breakfast or dinner, you can't have a meze without dips.

ROASTED OREGANO AND LEMON FETA

Preheat your oven to 200°C/gas mark 6. Place a 200g piece of feta in a small ovenproof dish and drizzle with olive oil. Finely slice ½ a lemon, pop it around the feta and sprinkle over ½ teaspoon of dried oregano (or a few sprigs of fresh oregano if you can find it). Season well and place in the oven for 20–25 minutes, until golden all over.

DRESSED TOMATO, RADISH AND POMEGRANATE

Peel and finely slice ½ a red onion and place in a mixing bowl with 2 tablespoons of red wine vinegar and a good pinch of sea salt and freshly ground black pepper. Toss together and leave to stand for 10 minutes. Meanwhile roughly chop 300g of ripe tomatoes and finely slice 6 radishes. Toss with the dressed onions, 1 heaped tablespoon of pomegranate seeds and a good drizzle of extra virgin olive oil. Rip over a handful of Greek basil or flat-leaf parsley leaves and serve.

A PLATE OF GRILLED HALLOUMI AND LOUNTZA

For both ingredients, simply thinly slice (½–1cm thick) and griddle on a hot, preheated griddle pan (or barbecue) until charred on both sides. Serve with a few wedges of lemon. (For those unfamiliar with lountza, it is Cypriot smoked pork tenderloin, and has the most wonderful aromatic flavour. It is marinated in red wine and smoked with coriander seeds and makes a great alternative to bacon. If you can't get hold of it, then by all means use smoked back bacon.)

EGGS

Breakfast eggs can vary, from strapatsada (on page 27), which are eggs scrambled into slow-cooked tomatoes, to eggs and greens, as described on page 31. Either dish would make a fantastic breakfast accompaniment, served straight to the table in a cast-iron pan. Having said that, there is equally nothing wrong with classic fried or boiled eggs. After Easter, when we always have an abundance of boiled eggs left over from dyeing, we'll simply eat those as part of our breakfast spread (and put them into everything and anything we can).

BREAD

An important part of any Cypriot meal. My favourite bread is koulouri, which is sesame-crusted and slightly sweet. But you'll also find that a round village-style loaf, pita breads (page 256) and flatbreads are widely eaten. If you are making brunch for many, have a selection of as many as you like/can find and have them piled up in a basket in the middle.

OTHER ESSENTIALS

- A bowl of thick Greek or Cypriot yoghurt is essential with most meals.
- Honey.
- A jar of (ideally homemade) jam.
- A plate of seasonal fruit.
- A vat of strong coffee, of course.

OTHER RECIPES THAT WOULD GO DOWN A TREAT

- Anari, pistachio and apricot pancake (page 42).
- Chocolate and halva marble cake (page 45).
- Spetsofai (page 166) – although not technically a breakfast dish, sausage cooked with peppers would make a wonderful start to the day.
- Marathopita (page 35)

Clockwise from top left: honey, yoghurt, eggs, houmous (page 57), roasted oregano and lemon feta (page 20), koulouri (page 257), grilled halloumi and lountza (page 21), tomato, radish and pomegranate (page 20), olives and pickles

TAHINI, BANANA AND HONEY *KOULOURI*

This recipe came about when we were island-hopping around the Greek islands, and it was our breakfast most mornings. With bread from the village bakery (there is always a bakery) and local honey, it is an easy yet delicious start to the day, and perfect for times of fasting.

SERVES 2

1 ripe banana
1 heaped tablespoon tahini
¼ teaspoon ground cinnamon
a pinch of sea salt
3 tablespoons honey
4 slices of bread, koulouri if possible
  (see page 257)
olive oil
1 tablespoon sesame seeds

Place a griddle pan on a high heat. In a bowl mash the banana, then add the tahini, cinnamon, sea salt and a drizzle of honey. You won't need too much honey, as you'll add more afterwards.

Drizzle the slices of bread with a little olive oil – this will be the outside of the sandwich. Turn them over, and spread the banana tahini on the undrizzled side of two of the slices. Top with the remaining two slices, so that the olive oil drizzle is facing upwards. Place the sandwiches on the hot griddle pan and put a weight on top to press them down. Griddle for 3–4 minutes, until nicely charred, then turn them over and griddle for a few minutes more. When they are ready, finish by drizzling each sandwich with a tablespoon of honey and sprinkling over the sesame seeds. Plate up, cut in half and tuck in.

SWEET TOMATO SCRAMBLED EGGS: *STRAPATSADA*

Further on in this chapter you will see that there is a whole page dedicated to Greeks' love of serving eggs with greens. This is usually an accompaniment to a main meal, or part of a meze. However, the egg love-fest doesn't stop there. Strapatsada is a meal in its own right, and works whatever the time of the day. It makes a wonderful brunch, but equally it is perfect for dinner when you are tired and don't have masses of time, or energy. The one thing I would say is don't be put off by the fact that there are so few ingredients. It is important to use ripe tomatoes, and cook the base for the stated time, and I promise you will be rewarded with a delicious simple meal.

SERVES 2

2 garlic cloves
500g ripe tomatoes
2 tablespoons olive oil
5 eggs
sea salt and freshly ground
   black pepper
¼ teaspoon dried oregano
a pinch of black onion seeds
50g feta, or a crumbly goat's cheese

Peel and finely chop the garlic. Peel and finely chop the tomatoes (see page 12 for peeling tomatoes). Place a medium frying pan on a medium heat and pour in the olive oil. Add the garlic, fry for a minute or until lightly golden, then add the tomatoes. Season well, gently bring to the boil, then reduce just a little and leave the tomatoes to cook for around 8–10 minutes. Most of the liquid needs to have evaporated and the tomatoes should start to gently caramelise.

Crack the eggs into the same bowl you grated your tomatoes in (who needs extra washing up?) and season well. Beat, then pour into the pan with the tomatoes. Lower the heat a little more and scramble the two ingredients together. Keep stirring and cooking over a low heat. When the eggs are just cooked, remove from the heat and sprinkle over the dried oregano and a pinch of black onion seeds. Crumble over the feta. Serve the strapatsada spooned over toast, with charred pita, or as part of a breakfast spread.

THE PANAYIOTOU HALLOUMI AND MINT BUNDT: *HALLOUMOPITA*

I've included this recipe here as opposed to in the sweet chapter, because even though it is a cake and it is baked, it isn't sweet per se. To be honest it isn't overtly savoury either, and can work in a multitude of situations – a slab for breakfast, an afternoon treat, even on the side of a bowl of soup instead of bread. If you like halloumi you must give this a try. Halloumi. Cake. Enough said.

SERVES 12

a knob of butter
250g self-raising flour, plus
   a little extra
6 sprigs of mint
250g halloumi
2 pieces of mastic and mehlepi
   (see page 17) (optional)
5 large eggs
125ml olive oil
200ml whole milk
2 teaspoons baking powder
¼ teaspoon ground cinnamon

Preheat your oven to 170°C/gas mark 3. Grease a bundt tin with the butter and dust with flour so it's completely coated, tapping out the excess.

Pick the mint leaves, finely chop and place in a large mixing bowl. Coarsely grate in the halloumi. Crush the mastic and mehlepi with a teaspoon of flour, until finely ground, and add to the bowl. Add the remaining ingredients and whisk everything together until well mixed. Pour the batter into the floured bundt tin and bake for 45 minutes, or until cooked through. Leave to cool in the tin for 5 minutes, then turn out on to a cooling rack and leave to cool completely.

GREENS AND EGGS, A LOVE AFFAIR: *HORTA ME AVGA*

Greens and eggs – sure, it's not a new concept; however, Greek people's love for seasonal greens cooked in eggs is unrivalled. Almost every meal at my Yiayia Maroulla's house would be adorned with a plate of some sort of vegetable cooked in eggs. Even on Christmas Day, there would be a plate of it on the table. It's not a recipe so much as an idea, a concept, and of course it can be embellished in any way you wish. But if I'm honest, in an age when eggs are usually finished with some sort of chilli sauce, a slice of avocado and other 'on trend' ingredients, the simplicity and respectfulness of a dish like this is so welcome.

SERVES 4

200g horta (see page 13) or
   200g chard or 4 large handfuls
   of whatever greens are in season
   – mix in things like dandelion
   leaves, amaranth, rocket, etc.
6 spring onions
4 garlic cloves
1 bunch of soft herbs – a mix
   of parsley, mint and/or dill
1 green chilli (optional)
olive oil
8 large eggs
sea salt and freshly ground
   black pepper
½ a lemon

Wash the greens incredibly well, to make sure there is no dirt left, and trim them. Roughly chop and leave to one side. Trim and slice the spring onions, peel and finely chop the garlic, and pick the herb leaves. If using, halve, deseed and finely chop the chilli.

Place 4 tablespoons of olive oil in a large frying pan and place on a medium-low heat. Add the spring onions and garlic and sauté for 3–4 minutes, until softened but not coloured. Add the washed and chopped greens to the pan, give it all a good stir, then cover with a lid and cook for 5 minutes, or until all the greens have softened and cooked down.

Meanwhile whisk the eggs in a large mixing bowl with a generous pinch of salt and pepper. Chop the picked herbs, add most of them to the eggs, and whisk together. When the greens are ready, pour the eggs into the saucepan and stir them into the greens. Cook gently until you have creamy scrambled eggs, then remove the pan from the heat. Squeeze over a little lemon, scatter over the remaining chopped herbs and the chopped chilli, and serve straight away.

A SOCRATOUS FAMILY FAVOURITE: HALLOUMI AND APRICOT JAM SANDWICHES

I cannot emphasise enough how much I love this combination. At first I thought it was down to nostalgia, but the more people I introduce it to, the more I know the Socratous clan are not alone. Of course the combination of salty and sweet isn't a new thing, and jam and cheese sandwiches are a widely-loved combination. But there is something specifically about the marriage of super-salty halloumi with the sweet, slight tartness of apricot jam that is nothing short of bliss. Basic, yes, but I urge you to give it a try – so much so that I have dedicated a page to it (and to my Uncle Dee, who came up with it). And it has to be white bread and there has to be butter – this is not a time to think about cutting calories or corners.

MAKES 1

3 slices of halloumi, about
   1½cm thick
2 slices of good-quality white bread
   (I love koulouri bread, Cypriot
   sesame bread, but any good
   white loaf will do)
unsalted butter
1–2 tablespoons of apricot jam
   (see page 36 to make your own, or
   just use good-quality shop-bought)

Place a griddle pan on a high heat, or preheat your grill to high. When it's hot, griddle or grill your halloumi slices for a couple of minutes on the first side, then for 1 minute on the second side. This will depend on whether you use a grill or a griddle. What you are looking for is a little colour on the cheese, either good char marks or a golden edge, and a soft pliable texture – it shouldn't be rubbery or too firm.

While the halloumi is grilling, place the bread in the toaster or under the grill and toast until lightly golden. Remove, butter one side of each slice and top with a good layer of apricot jam. When the halloumi is ready, transfer it straight to one of the slices of toast, top with the other and give it a gentle press together. Cut in half and tuck in straight away (it's no good waiting, or the halloumi will go cold). Bliss.

FENNEL STUFFED FLATBREADS: *MARATHOPITA*

I love the little pitoues (little stuffed baked breads) my yiayia often makes, and it was recommended that I try them with fennel. Unlike the olive and halloumi varieties I have grown up with, these bad boys are pan-fried, which may be why I love them all the more. As wild, herby fennel is not easy to buy or find over here, I have added spinach and dill to give a similar texture and flavour. Also, I have given the option to add feta, because it just works so well, but of course you can leave it out for a true Lenten experience. I hope you love these as much as I do.

MAKES 8–10

400g strong bread flour
½ teaspoon sea salt, plus a little extra
100ml olive oil, plus extra for frying
1 tablespoon red or white wine
vinegar
½ a bulb of fennel
4 spring onions
50g baby spinach
a good pinch of freshly ground
black pepper
a few sprigs of dill
50g feta (optional)
olive oil

Start by making the dough. Whisk together the flour, salt, olive oil and vinegar. Add around 200ml of cold water, then bring it together with your hands and knead it until smooth, adding more water if needed if it is a little dry. Dust a clean worktop with a little flour, then turn out the dough and knead for around 5 minutes. You know it's ready when you poke the dough and it springs back. Return to a clean bowl, cover with a tea towel and leave to rest for 45 minutes.

Meanwhile, trim and finely slice the fennel and spring onions. Place in a colander with the spinach, a pinch of salt and a good pinch of pepper. Scrunch everything together with your hands and leave in the sink to drain.

When the dough and filling are ready, turn the dough out onto a lightly floured surface and cut into 10 even pieces. Squeeze the spinach mixture one last time to remove any moisture and transfer to a mixing bowl. Finely chop the dill and stir through. Crumble in the feta if using.

Flatten out a piece of dough so it is just big enough to pile in 1 heaped tablespoon of the fennel mixture. Hold the dough in the palm of your hand, spoon in the filling, then pinch the dough over the top so it is completely enclosed. Place the filled dough on a floured worktop and flatten with your hand, then roll out lightly so it is around ½–1cm thick. Repeat with the rest of the dough and the filling.

Place a large frying pan on a medium heat and drizzle in a few table-spoons of olive oil. Fry the stuffed breads for around 2–3 minutes on each side, until golden and crisp, then serve. Ideally you'll eat them warm, but if you have leftovers they are still great the next day – just warm them in a pan or in the oven slightly first if you can.

APRICOT JAM

Apricots are one of my favourite fruits, I love them in all their guises: straight up, in tarts, torn up in salads, with apricot jam being my all time favourite preserve. The beauty of this recipe is that if you are a jam-making novice then this is the one for you. It is straightforward with no need for straining or thermometers. You could even leave out extracting the kernel if that scares you, however it is worth attempting for that extra almond-like flavour.

MAKES JUST UNDER 1KG

1kg apricots
600g granulated sugar
2 lemons
1 bay leaf

Halve the apricots, keeping 6 of the stones to one side, and place the flesh in a large heavy-bottomed saucepan. Add the sugar, the juice of the lemons and the bay leaf, and give everything a good stir. Leave to one side to steep for a couple of hours.

Using a nutcracker, or a rolling pin (be careful though), crack the 6 reserved apricot stones and remove the kernels. I find it easiest to place the stones in a tea towel before hitting, to stop them rolling around. Place the kernels in a small bowl and cover with boiling water, for just enough time to remove the brown paper skins. Split each kernel in half and add to the pan of fruit.

After 2 hours, place the pan on a low heat and stir until all the sugar has dissolved. Then turn the heat up to medium-high and cook for around 25–30 minutes, stirring often. You want the apricot flesh to have cooked down and to have a lovely deep golden colour – it'll be a medium soft set jam.

When the jam is ready, leave it to cool for 10 minutes, then carefully spoon into sterilised jars (try and make sure you get at least one apricot kernel in each jar). Seal while still hot, then leave to cool before labelling them. Once you've opened a jar, remember to store it in the fridge.

MOSPHILO JAM

The most Cypriot of all jams – this stuff is like liquid gold. It glows, it's smooth, it has the texture of golden syrup and it tastes like crab apples mixed with honey. For years none of us knew what mosphilo was in English. Relatives would show us these little fruits, like mini apples, and our faces would be blank. We now know they are a type of azarole or Mediterranean medlar. They are able to grow without water in harsh terrain, which is perfect for Cyprus over the very dry and hot summer months. It will forever remind me of my Great Uncle Taki, who lived in the house behind ours in Limassol. He passed away last year, but even in his 80s, come the autumn, he would make countless jars of mosphilo jam and sell them to all the neighbours. I would always be sent back to the UK with a jar for each member of the family. We would cherish it until we returned the following year.

MAKES AROUND 1KG

1kg mosphila (or azaroles or medlars)
1kg granulated sugar
3 large or 5 small scented geranium leaves (kioulli in Greek) (optional)
1 lemon

Place a small plate in the freezer. Place the mosphila in a large saucepan and cover with about 2 litres of water. Bring to the boil, then reduce to a simmer and cook for about 1 hour, until the fruit is tender and the liquid has reduced by around half. Skim off any scum that rises to the surface, and discard.

Strain the liquid through a fine sieve or muslin and discard the fruit (or you could use it to make a compote or pudding). Measure the remaining liquid – you should have around 800ml. Pour it into the cleaned pan and add the same volume of sugar. Add the geranium leaves, if using, and squeeze in the juice of the lemon. Bring to the boil, then reduce to a simmer. After 10 minutes, remove the geranium leaves, then continue to cook for a further 20 minutes, or until the jam has reached setting point. You can check this by spooning a little jam on to the frozen plate – it should feel like jelly when you run your finger through it.

Leave to cool for a few minutes, then spoon the jam into sterilised jars, leaving a 1cm gap at the top. Seal with the lids, then turn upside down to vacuum seal. Leave to cool completely and store until needed.

APPLE AND OLIVE OIL BREAKFAST CAKE

You'll find two apple cakes in this book: this one, which is a traditional style cake that most people are familiar with, and milopita (see page 230), which is more like a pie and for which most families have an inherited recipe. This one feels less like pudding, and is an acceptable sweet breakfast choice.

SERVES 12

a knob of butter
3 eating apples, about 375g in weight
1 tablespoon ground cinnamon
½ teaspoon mixed spice
325g caster sugar
375g self-raising flour
1 teaspoon baking powder
a good pinch of fine sea salt
4 large eggs
200ml olive oil
80ml apple or orange juice
1–2 tablespoons icing sugar

Grease a 23cm springform cake tin with the butter and line the bottom with greaseproof paper. Preheat your oven to 180°C/gas mark 4.

Peel and core the apples. Cut them into 1–1½cm pieces and place in a mixing bowl with the cinnamon, mixed spice and 25g of the caster sugar. Leave to one side.

In a large mixing bowl whisk together the flour, baking powder, sea salt and the remaining 300g of caster sugar. Make a well in the centre and crack in the eggs, then pour in the olive oil and fruit juice. Whisk everything until it has just come together, then pour half the mixture into the cake tin. Evenly spoon over two-thirds of the apple mixture. Top with the remaining cake mixture, then finish with the remaining apple, and any juices left in the bottom of the bowl. Pop the cake into the oven and bake for 1 hour–1 hour and 10 minutes, until cooked through.

Leave to cool in the tin for 10 minutes, then transfer to a cooling rack. Sift over the icing sugar and serve.

ANARI, PISTACHIO AND APRICOT PANCAKE

Anari, or Greek ricotta, is the base of so many sweet Greek dishes, and has (universally) become very popular in the form of a breakfast pancake. I felt inspired to use it to make a Cypriot summer breakfast, along with sweet apricots, which are plentiful in the early summer months. However feel free to change the fruit depending on the season, griddled pears would work well, as would segments of sweet oranges.

SERVES 2

125g fresh anari, or ricotta
100ml milk
2 large eggs
½ a lemon
60g caster sugar
a good pinch of sea salt
60g plain flour
½ teaspoon baking powder
30g unsalted butter
3–4 apricots
20g pistachios
2 sprigs of mint
2 tablespoons honey

Preheat your oven to 180°C/gas mark 4.

If using ricotta, drain it in a sieve to dry it out a little. Spoon the anari or strained ricotta into a large mixing bowl and pour in the milk. Separate the eggs, adding the yolks to the ricotta and keeping the whites to one side in a clean medium-sized mixing bowl. Finely grate the lemon zest into the ricotta, add the sugar and salt and beat all the ingredients together. Sift in the flour and baking powder and fold them in.

Whisk the egg whites with an electric hand whisk until you have stiff peaks, then fold them into the ricotta batter, keeping it as light and airy as possible.

Place a medium non-stick ovenproof frying pan on a medium heat and add the butter. As soon as it has melted and is bubbling, ladle in the ricotta batter, then place the pan in the oven. Bake for 20–25 minutes, until risen, gold and the edges are crisp.

Meanwhile place a griddle pan on a high heat. Cut the apricots into wedges and, when the griddle is hot, grill them for a few minutes on each side until charred. Finely chop the pistachios. Pick the mint leaves.

When the pancake is ready, slide it on to a serving plate or board. Top with the apricot wedges, drizzle with honey, scatter over the pistachios and mint leaves and tuck in.

VERMICELLI IN MILK: *FIDE ME TO GALA*

This is possibly the simplest recipe in the book, and one that is filled with nostalgia for me: my mum and maternal grandparents' breakfast of choice in cold weather. It is such a comforting and homely recipe.

If the idea of pasta cooked in milk is baffling, think of this as a Cypriot porridge or rice pudding. Treat it in the same way: eat it simply, sweetened, as we do. Or alternatively feel free to embellish it with dried or fresh fruits, or nuts, or try infusing the milk with saffron or cardamom (my favourite).

SERVES 1

a small knob of unsalted butter
50g vermicelli
400ml milk
a small stick of cinnamon, a clove
    or a pinch of saffron (optional)
1–2 tablespoons granulated sugar
raisins, fruits, nuts, etc. to garnish
    (optional)

Put the butter into a small saucepan and place on a medium heat. Crush in the vermicelli, so it is in small pieces, and fry for a few minutes, until it starts to turn golden. Pour in the milk, add any flavourings you might like, and stir in 1 tablespoon of the sugar. Bring to the boil, then simmer for around 5–8 minutes, or until cooked through and creamy, stirring occasionally.

Taste, add more sugar if needed, then leave to cool and thicken for 5 minutes. Serve with any garnishes you may be using.

CHOCOLATE, TAHINI AND HALVA MARBLE CAKE

As I mentioned in my introduction on page 20, when I was growing up breakfast was a couple of slices of cake and a glass of milk. This was always my favourite. A very Mediterranean thing indeed!

SERVES 8–10

225g unsalted butter, at room
   temperature, plus extra for greasing
50g dark chocolate
225g caster sugar
4 large eggs
225g self-raising flour
1 teaspoon vanilla extract
3 tablespoons milk
1 tablespoon tahini
a good pinch of sea salt
50g halva (either shop-bought
   or homemade, recipe overleaf)

Preheat your oven to 180°C/gas mark 4. Grease a 2lb loaf tin with butter and line it with greaseproof paper.

Break the chocolate into pieces and melt, either in the microwave, or in a heatproof bowl over a pan of simmering water. Stir until just melted, then leave to one side to cool a little.

Put the butter and sugar into a large bowl and beat (either by hand or with an electric mixer) until pale and fluffy. Beat in the eggs, flour, vanilla extract and 2 tablespoons of milk until smooth. Spoon half the mixture into a second bowl. Add the tahini to one of the bowls and beat in. Into the other bowl mix the remaining tablespoon of milk, the salt and the melted chocolate.

Alternate large spoonfuls of each mixture in the loaf tin, layering them up, then ripple them all together using the end of a knife. Crumble over the halva and place in the oven for 50 minutes, until golden and cooked through. If it is still a little undercooked, return it to the oven for 10 minutes, until a skewer comes out clean. Leave to cool in the tin for 10 minutes, then transfer to a cooling rack.

HOMEMADE HALVA

I could give you thermometer readings to get the perfect temperature for your sugar syrup, but it can be off-putting, and to be honest this is a very forgiving recipe – I've made it countless times without. Not everything needs to be over-complicated: just make sure your syrup is thick and golden and you'll be absolutely fine.

MAKES PLENTY!

olive oil
175g caster sugar
250g tahini
a pinch of ground cinnamon
½ teaspoon good-quality
  vanilla extract

Line the base of a 23cm cake tin with greaseproof paper and grease the sides with a little oil.

Place the sugar in a medium saucepan with 70ml of water and gently bring to the boil over a medium heat. Do not stir, just swirl the pan, otherwise the sugar will crystallise. Once it starts to bubble, reduce the heat to low and leave to simmer for around 12–15 minutes, until you have a thick, golden syrup. Remove from the heat and leave to one side for 5 minutes.

Meanwhile warm the tahini in a small pan with the cinnamon and vanilla extract. Do not let it burn or boil. When it is just warm, spoon it into the sugar syrup and quickly beat the two together to make a smooth paste. This is best done with a wooden spoon or spatula. As soon as it is smooth, spoon it into the lined tin and leave to cool. Once cool, cover the tin and transfer to the fridge to set overnight. It is then ready to eat or cook with.

2

MEZE

Clockwise from top: houmous (page 57), tirokafteri (page 56), tzatziki, skordalia (page 61), melitzanosalata (page 60)

MAMA'S TZATZIKI AKA *TALATTOURI*

My mum is an incredible cook and has a vast repertoire of dishes. However, this is one of the things I associate with her most: proper Greek tzatziki, or, as we call it, talattouri. She always makes it in abundance whenever we are having a family celebration or party, and mine is just never as good. The cucumber is salted and drained, a small step but a key one, as it gives you an intensely creamy dip – it shouldn't be at all runny.

SERVES 4–6

1 cucumber
sea salt and freshly ground
   black pepper
1 small garlic clove
1 teaspoon dried mint
500g Greek yoghurt
extra virgin olive oil
½ a lemon

Start by draining the cucumber. Trim it and coarsely grate it into a mixing bowl. Mix in 1 teaspoon of flaky sea salt (if using fine sea salt, use ½ teaspoon), then spoon it into a clean, fine sieve. Leave it to drain over the mixing bowl for 1 hour, stirring occasionally to remove all the liquid. When it is ready, spoon it into a larger mixing bowl. Finely grate in the peeled garlic clove and add the dried mint and a good pinch of ground black pepper.

Spoon the yoghurt into the fine sieve. You don't want to press it through, just to remove any excess liquid. When it's drained, spoon it into the bowl with the grated cucumber, drizzle in 2 tablespoons of extra virgin olive oil, squeeze in a little lemon juice to taste and mix everything together well. Serve finished with a little drizzle of oil on top and sprinkled with a little extra dried mint.

SPICY WHIPPED FETA WITH CUMIN: *TIROKAFTERI*

This is a slightly bastardised version of tirokafteri, in that I have enhanced it a little with cumin. It is my Cypriot twist on a much-loved classic. Serve this as part of a meze, or as an appetiser before a meal with a pile of warm flatbreads, or even better as part of a souvlaki feast. It's a dream on a hot flatbread, topped with skewers of barbecued pork and salad (see page 154).

SERVES 4–6

1–2 green chillies
1 garlic clove
1 teaspoon cumin seeds
75ml olive oil
200g feta
250g ricotta
75g Greek yoghurt
½ a lemon
sea salt and freshly ground
    black pepper

Halve, deseed and finely slice the chillies, and peel and finely chop the garlic. Lightly crush the cumin seeds. Pour the oil into a small frying pan or saucepan. Add the chilli, garlic and cumin and fry for just a minute or two, until the garlic and chilli are lightly golden. Remove from the heat and leave to cool.

Crumble the feta and ricotta into a food processor, spoon in the Greek yoghurt and squeeze in the lemon juice. Spoon in half the chilli, garlic and cumin oil, and pulse everything together. You can blitz until smooth, or leave it a little chunkier, which is how I like it. Season to taste, and add a little more lemon if it needs a bit more acidity. Spoon the dip into your serving bowl or plate, drizzle with the remaining spiced oil, and serve.

HOUMOUS

Houmous is such a personal thing and this will undoubtedly cause some controversy, as everyone has their own way of making it and claims on its origin. This is how I make mine: it yields a creamier, mousse-like texture that is influenced by another Cypriot dip called 'tashi' – tahini. Tashi has all the same ingredients as houmous, just minus the chickpeas, and (funnily enough) needs a tonne of tahini. When it comes to houmous – personally I think you can taste the difference when you cook your own chickpeas; however, I have also given you instructions for using tinned. The one thing I would say is, if you have to use tinned, please please please use the best quality chickpeas you can find. Or even better, ones that come in a jar and look deliciously plump.

SERVES 6–8

250g dried chickpeas and
  3 teaspoons bicarbonate of soda
OR 2 × 400g tins of organic
  chickpeas
2 garlic cloves
1–2 lemons
100g tahini
sea salt
extra virgin olive oil
sweet smoked paprika, to serve

If you are cooking your own chickpeas, check out the recipe on page 16 for instructions. Leave them in their cooking liquor to cool down.

Whether using dried or tinned, start by draining the chickpeas but keep the liquid. Peel the garlic cloves and finely grate into a food processor and squeeze in the juice of 1 lemon. Add the tahini and a good splash of the chickpea liquor and blitz until you have a loose, pale paste. Add the drained chickpeas and a generous pinch of salt and blitz until creamy. Taste, add more salt and lemon if need be, and if it feels a little thick and grainy add a splash more water (not too much though, or you'll end up with a sloppy mess – it should be light and mousse-like). Serve spooned on to a plate, drizzled with extra virgin olive oil and sprinkled with paprika.

CHARRED AUBERGINE, GARLIC AND PARSLEY: *MELITZANOSALATA*

This is my take on melitzanosalata and I really think it sings. If you are lighting a barbecue, now is a perfect time to make it for the best smoky flavour. Alternatively you can of course cook the aubergines in the oven as described below, or, even better, over an open flame; however, be warned that it does make a bit of a mess. Yiayia Maroulla would line her hob with foil. It might look slightly mental but trust me, blistered aubergines release a lot of liquid and can be a nightmare to clean afterwards.

SERVES 6–8

4 large aubergines
sea salt and freshly ground
    black pepper
½ a bunch of flat-leaf parsley
50g fresh white breadcrumbs
1–2 lemons
1–2 garlic cloves
100ml extra virgin olive oil
40g feta (optional)
½ teaspoon sweet smoked paprika
    or sumac

If cooking the aubergines in the oven, preheat it to 200°C/gas mark 6. Place them in a large roasting tray and cook for around an hour, turning every 20 minutes until evenly charred all over. Alternatively you can do this on the barbecue under the grill or even over an open flame (see introduction). Turn the aubergines until the skin is blistered and cooked through. When they are ready, leave to one side until cool enough to handle.

When they have cooled a little but are still warm, peel the aubergines using your hands – you should be able to peel away the skins – then roughly chop the flesh and place in a colander. Sprinkle over a teaspoon of sea salt, mix together well, and leave in the sink or over a clean bowl for around 30 minutes, to remove any excess liquid.

Meanwhile pick the parsley leaves and finely chop. Place the breadcrumbs in a large mixing bowl and squeeze over the juice of 1 of the lemons. Peel and finely grate in the garlic cloves. When the aubergine is ready, transfer it to the bowl of breadcrumb mixture and mash it all together with a fork. Keep going until smooth but still with a bit of texture (you can do this in a food processor for a very smooth dip, but I prefer mine to have a bit more of a bite to it). Slowly pour in the oil and keep mashing, then season with black pepper and stir in the chopped parsley leaves. Taste and check the seasoning, adding more lemon, salt or pepper if needed. Leave the melitzanosalata covered in the fridge for at least 1 hour before serving, so the flavours have a chance to mix and settle. Then serve drizzled with a little extra virgin olive oil, the feta crumbled over the top (if using) and sprinkled with the paprika or sumac.

TOASTED WALNUT AND BEAN SKORDALIA: *KARYDIA ME FASOLIA SKORDALIA*

Skordalia can vary in terms of what thickens it – it can be potato, bread or beans. But the one thing that stays the same is the punchy garlic element – skorda meaning garlic in Greek. It's not for the faint-hearted but it makes a wonderful accompaniment to most dishes and meze spreads. It is fabulous served alongside simply grilled fish, meats and even vegetables. I even love a spoonful of it rippled into soups and stews.

SERVES 8

100g walnuts
4 garlic cloves
1 × 400g tin of white beans –
  cannellini or butter beans work well
150ml olive oil
1 lemon
sea salt and freshly ground
  black pepper

Preheat your oven to 180°C/gas mark 4. Place the walnuts on a small tray and pop them into the oven for 8–10 minutes, until lightly golden. Remove and leave to one side to cool. When they are ready, place most of them in a food processor. Peel and add the garlic and blitz everything until finely ground.

Drain the beans (reserving the juice), add to the food processor and purée until smooth. With the motor still running, slowly pour in the olive oil, feeding it into the purée gradually. If you don't have a food processor you can do this by hand or with a pestle and mortar. When it is all incorporated, squeeze in the juice of the lemon and add enough of the bean juice to make it smooth and creamy. Season to taste.

Chop the remaining walnuts and garnish on top of the dip.

From top: roasted coriander mushrooms
(page 65), htipiti (page 64), taramasalata

YIAYIA MARTHA'S FAMOUS TARAMA: *TARAMASALATA*

If you are about to dismiss this recipe based on your experiences of the acrid pink taramasalata bought in supermarkets, I implore you to stop and rethink. Properly made tarama is a beautiful thing. It should be delicately balanced, pale in colour and moreish (having said that, I know plenty of people who love the pink stuff, me included). My Yiayia Martha is famous for hers, and she would always make it fresh in the restaurant, keeping the regulars (and family) hooked. It is so addictive that one Christmas Day my sister famously ate twelve roast potatoes dipped in my yiayia's tarama – after her Christmas dinner. She's on to something, to be fair – the salty, acidic tarama is a dream when teamed with a hot, crispy roast potato. Alternatively you can of course serve it the traditional way with fresh bread and crunchy crudités; we particularly love it with radishes.

N.B. I have had to tweak my yiayia's recipe, as the roe she buys isn't widely available; however, I hope this comes close.

SERVES 6–8

200g salted cod or mullet roe
  (or smoked if you can't get salted)
200g white bread, crusts removed
½ an onion
1 teaspoon ground white pepper
2–3 lemons
100ml light olive oil (not extra virgin)
150ml vegetable oil
a plate of crisp radishes, black olives
  and koulouri bread (see page 257),
  to serve

If using smoked roe, soak it in cold water for a couple of hours to ease the smokiness.

Cut the bread into large chunks and place it in a large bowl. Cover completely with cold water and leave to soak for a few seconds. Gently squeeze out the excess water and transfer the bread to a food processor.

Drain the cod's roe and peel off the outer layer. Add the roe to the processor bowl. Peel and coarsely grate in the onion. Add the white pepper, squeeze in the juice of 2 of the lemons and blitz everything for 1–2 minutes, until smooth. With the motor still running very slowly, pour in both the oils in a steady stream. If your food processor doesn't have a feeding tube, or if you are making this in a pestle and mortar (which is also possible), add the oil a couple of tablespoons at a time.

When the oils have all been completely added, have a taste and tweak the seasoning, adding more lemon juice if needed. Spoon the tarama into a small plate or bowl, top with black olives and drizzle with a little olive oil. Serve with a plate of crisp radishes and chunks of fresh koulouri.

ROASTED RED PEPPER, CHILLI AND FETA: *HTIPITI*

This is more of a Greek recipe than a Cypriot one – I know this because I made it recently and my yiayia loved it so much she asked for the recipe. This is pretty epic, as I'm sure you have sussed out already that my yiayia is a Cypriot food oracle. Pleased to say it's very easy, impressive, and if you use jarred peppers it is also incredibly quick.

SERVES 4–6

2 large or 3 medium red peppers
    (or 300g roasted red peppers
    in olive oil)
1 small garlic clove
1 red chilli
250g feta
extra virgin olive oil
freshly ground black pepper
½ a lemon

If you are blackening your own peppers, place them directly over a gas hob, and turn them every 5 minutes or so, until blackened all over. Place in a large bowl and cover with a plate, or cling film, for 5 minutes so the steam loosens the blackened skin. Remove the peppers, and flake away the skin with your fingers. Halve and remove the seeds.

Peel the garlic and finely chop or finely grate onto a large board. Halve, deseed and finely chop the chilli. Chop the charred peppers, working in the already chopped garlic and chilli, until everything is fine but not a puree.

Break the feta into a large bowl and mash it up with a fork. Stir in the red pepper mixture, and enough olive oil to bind it all together. Season with freshly ground black pepper and squeeze in a little lemon juice, to taste.

MUSHROOMS ROASTED IN CORIANDER AND WINE:
MANITARIA ME KOLIANDRO KAI KRASI

You'll often find a bowl of simply cooked mushrooms in a Cypriot meze; a welcome addition after the endless stream of rich plates. (You find vast amounts of wild mushrooms in Cyprus during late autumn.) I've jazzed them up a little here, by roasting them, and love the slight char you get from the oven. Don't be put off by the amount of coriander seeds – trust me, it works.

SERVES 4–6

600g closed cup mushrooms
1 tablespoon coriander seeds
4 garlic cloves
olive oil
½ a bunch of thyme
sea salt and freshly ground
   black pepper
100ml dry white wine
½ a bunch of flat-leaf parsley
4 spring onions
½ a lemon

Preheat the oven to 190°C/gas mark 5. Wipe the mushrooms clean and cut them into evenly-sized pieces, leaving some whole, some halved. Transfer to a snug roasting tray (you want the mushrooms to be spread out in one layer but don't worry if they're a little cramped, they'll shrink as they cook). Crush the coriander seeds in a pestle and mortar – but not too fine, it's nice for them to still have a little texture. Lightly crush the garlic cloves, skin still on, with the side of your knife.

Sprinkle the coriander over the mushrooms and drizzle everything with olive oil. Pick over the thyme leaves. Season generously and add the crushed garlic cloves. Toss everything together well and spread out into one layer. Pour over the white wine and place in the oven for around 40 minutes, stirring once or twice, until the wine has evaporated and the mushrooms are golden and a little roasted. If they're not quite golden, leave them in the oven for a further 5 minutes.

While the mushrooms are roasting, pick and crudely chop the parsley leaves. Trim and slice the spring onions and toss them with the parsley leaves, then squeeze over the lemon juice.

When the mushrooms are ready, leave them to one side to cool for 5 minutes, then toss in the parsley mixture. You can serve them straight away or, alternatively, leave them to cool and serve at room temperature.

Clockwise from top: gigantes (page 117), roasted beets (page 69), fried halloumi, fava (page 67)

FAVA, PICKLED ONIONS WITH CAPERS

Fava is easily one of my favourite Greek mezedes – along with a Greek salad and a plate of calamari I am really quite content. My cousin Cassie introduced me to the addition of rosemary and I am so glad she did: it adds a lovely earthiness to the purée. Also the addition of green harissa is totally untraditional and I am sure there are Greeks everywhere tutting at me right now, but it does work and makes a wonderful change. However, if you want it totally traditional, simply leave it out.

SERVES 6

300g yellow split peas
2 onions
2 garlic cloves
extra virgin olive oil
4 sprigs of rosemary
1 bay leaf
1 red onion
2 lemons
sea salt and freshly ground
    black pepper
2 tablespoons capers
a couple of tablespoons of
    green harissa (optional)

Place the yellow split peas in a sieve and rinse under running water.

Peel and finely chop the 2 onions and the garlic. Place a large saucepan on a medium-low heat, pour in 3 tablespoons of olive oil and add the chopped veg to the pan. Pick in the rosemary leaves, then gently sauté for 10 minutes, until soft and sticky but not coloured. Stir the washed split peas into the pan, add the bay leaf and pour in 1 litre of boiling water. Turn the heat up, bring to the boil, then reduce the heat to low and cover with a lid. Cook gently for around 40 minutes, until the water has all been absorbed and the fava is rich and creamy (check during cooking and spoon off any scum that comes to the surface, and top up with more boiling water if needed – don't let it cook dry, it needs to be creamy).

While the fava is cooking, peel and finely slice the red onion. Squeeze over the juice of half a lemon and leave to one side to soften.

When the fava is ready, discard the bay leaf, season generously and use a stick blender to blitz to a smooth purée, adding a splash of boiling water to loosen, if need be. Squeeze in the juice of the remaining 1½ lemons and pour in a couple of tablespoons of extra virgin olive oil. Beat it all together. Serve the creamy fava topped with a spoonful of dressed sliced onions and capers, and the green harissa, if using.

FRIED HALLOUMI, MINT AND ALMONDS

As part of a traditional Cypriot meze, halloumi is often served simply cooked on the BBQ, at a push it may get a drizzle of honey – but that really is a push. As wonderful as that is, sometimes it's nice to mix things up and give this versatile much-loved cheese a new lease of life. I love pairing it with mint, which can often be found in halloumi itself, depending on the maker. And I haven't included honey in this recipe, as I am conscious of being a honey bore, however if you did drizzle a little over at the end then that would be no bad thing.

SERVES 4

50g almonds
olive oil
½ tablespoon sesame seeds
sea salt and freshly ground
   black pepper
6 sprigs of mint
250g halloumi
½ a lemon

Preheat the oven to 200°C/gas mark 6. Roughly chop the almonds and toss with a little olive oil, the sesame seeds and a good pinch of salt and pepper. Spread out on a baking tray and pop into the oven for 10 minutes, until golden. Remove and leave to one side to cool. Pick the mint leaves and roughly chop, then, when the nuts and seeds are cool, toss through the mint leaves.

Cut the halloumi into 1cm slices. Place a large non-stick frying pan on a medium heat and pour in enough olive oil to lightly cover the base. Fry the halloumi slices for a couple of minutes on each side, until golden all over. Serve straight away, with the roasted nut and mint mixture sprinkled on top, and the lemon, cut into wedges.

ROASTED BEETS AND LEAVES WITH DILL YOGHURT:
PANTZARI ME ANITHO GIAOURTI

Beetroot might not feel quintessentially Cypriot but you'd be surprised, you'll always find it in Greek and Cypriot grocers, and often it'll be cooked whole, still in its skin. If that is the case, buy it like that and skip the first part of this recipe. You sacrifice using the delicious leaves, but it does make the recipe a lot easier and quicker. Simply peel them by flaking the skin away with your hands and go from there.

SERVES 6–8

1kg beetroots, with their tops
olive oil
sea salt and freshly ground
    black pepper
6 garlic cloves
1 tablespoon red wine vinegar
½ a bunch of dill
250g Greek yoghurt
1 lemon
2 teaspoons capers

Remove the beetroot leaves and keep to one side. Place the beetroots in a large saucepan and cover with water. Bring to the boil over a high heat, then reduce the heat slightly and simmer for around 45 minutes, until almost cooked through. Meanwhile preheat the oven to 190°C/gas mark 5.

Remove the beets from the pan, let them cool until you are able to handle them without burning yourself, then peel off the skin. Chop them into even chunks, around 4cm in size, and place in a large roasting tray. Drizzle over enough olive oil to lightly coat, then season and toss everything together. Arrange in one even layer and place in the oven for 20 minutes.

Remove from the oven, sprinkle over the garlic cloves and drizzle over the red wine vinegar. Toss the beetroot leaves with a little olive oil, just enough to coat, and pop them into the tray also, draping them over some of the beetroot. Put back into the oven for 20–30 minutes, until the beetroot is caramelised and cooked through, and the leaves are crisp. When ready, leave to one side to cool to room temperature.

While the beetroot is cooling, make the yoghurt dressing. Finely chop the dill and add most of it to the yoghurt along with the finely grated zest and juice of the lemon, a generous pinch of salt and pepper and 2 tablespoons of olive oil. Spoon the yoghurt over a serving platter, then pile over the roasted beetroot, garlic cloves and leaves. Scatter over the capers and the remaining dill and serve.

A STORY ABOUT WATERMELON AND HALLOUMI

Apologies in advance about the simplistic title. I was torn with this one, as it isn't a recipe but more a heads-up. You see, watermelon and feta is quite the done thing, popping up regularly in salads, on menus and in magazines everywhere, and it is a wonderful combination. The sweet cool watermelon, the salty, creamy, slightly tangy feta – they are a dream. However, I'd just like to promote the idea of halloumi and watermelon. In Cyprus it is as standard as having tonic with your gin. During the summer, when everyone is a little too hot to cook, or to eat anything too heavy, slices of halloumi will be served up with chunks of chilled watermelon as an afternoon snack. It isn't frilly or fancy, we don't make it into a salad or garnish it with anything particularly photogenic. It is purely two complementary ingredients, devoured together. The only requirement here, as with most things but especially here, is the quality of your ingredients. Watermelons are in season during the summer, when they are dense and sweet. Don't be tempted out of season, as they will be watery and insipid. And the halloumi – the real reason behind this epic chat. Halloumi is widely thought of as a 'rubbery' cheese, and in the UK I would say this is pretty accurate – the stuff that is sold in supermarkets leaves much to be desired (I wouldn't touch it un-grilled). However, good-quality halloumi is heavenly when eaten un-grilled or uncooked. It should be creamy, salty, flavoursome. You should be able to see and feel the layers. Yes, it is firm enough to grill, but it shouldn't be the equivalent of eating an eraser. Thankfully there are producers now making proper Cypriot halloumi in the UK (check out the suppliers on page 298), which I cannot recommend enough. Alternatively hunt down an international supermarket that imports the good stuff. Then treat yourself to an afternoon in the sun with a plate of these two harmoniously matched ingredients.

HONEY ROASTED ANARI WITH FIGS: *ANARI STO FOURNO ME SIKA*

I love anari every which way – sweet, savoury, straight up. Prepared like this it makes a great starter for a relaxed dinner with friends, and is incredibly simple to make. I'd suggest hunting down fresh anari or ricotta from a Mediterranean or Middle Eastern deli if you can; however, let's be realistic – if you can't, don't worry. Supermarket-bought ricotta will work fine, it's just a little wetter than the fresh stuff, so be sure to drain off any excess liquid.

SERVES 8

1 unwaxed lemon
6 sprigs of thyme or oregano
sea salt and freshly ground
   black pepper
extra virgin olive oil
4 bay leaves
1 × 500g round of fresh anari
   or ricotta (or 2 × 250g rounds)
8 figs
2 tablespoons honey
koulouri bread (see page 257)
   or ciabatta, to serve
4 garlic cloves

Preheat your oven to 200°C/gas mark 6. Remove the zest of the lemon in thick strips and place in a mortar with the thyme or oregano. Crush together lightly with a good pinch of salt and pepper and drizzle in a good glug of olive oil. Place the bay leaves in a small baking dish, just large enough to hold the cheese. Place the anari or ricotta on top of the bay leaves, and rub with the herb dressing. Slice the lemon quite thinly and scatter in the tray, on and around the anari. Halve and quarter the figs and nestle them around it also.

Pop the dish into the oven and roast for around 20 minutes, until the cheese becomes golden and tinged around the edges. Remove from the oven, drizzle with a couple of spoonfuls of honey and place back in the oven for a further 10–15 minutes.

While your cheese is finishing in the oven, start toasting your slices of koulouri. As soon as each slice is ready, cut the garlic cloves in half, rub the bread with the cut side and drizzle with extra virgin olive oil.

Serve a stack of toasts with the hot roasted anari, lots of knives, and let everyone tuck in.

GRILLED SPICY PRAWNS WITH FETA AND OUZO: *GARITHES SAGANAKI*

We're always told seafood and cheese are a no-no, but this recipe just goes to show they can be a match made in heaven. Make sure you serve it with plenty of bread for mopping up the juices – the prawns almost feel incidental once you've eaten what's left in the dish.

SERVES 4

500g king prawns, butterflied
1 onion
4 garlic cloves
1 red chilli
½ a bunch of flat-leaf parsley
4 ripe tomatoes
50ml olive oil
½ teaspoon paprika
50ml ouzo
1 tablespoon tomato purée
sea salt and freshly ground
   black pepper
125g feta

When you butterfly the prawns, remove the vein. Ideally do this leaving the tails on, but if it's easier to remove them, that's fine too. Peel and finely chop the onion and garlic. Halve, deseed and finely slice the chilli. Pick and finely chop the parsley leaves. Peel the tomatoes (see page 12) and finely chop the flesh – you can coarsely grate them if easier.

Pour the olive oil into a large frying pan, and pop on to a medium-low heat. Add the onion, garlic and chilli and sauté for 15 minutes. Stir in the paprika and the ouzo – be careful, as it may flambé/catch light. Leave it to cook away for a minute, then add the tomato purée and season well. Stir for a minute, then add the chopped tomatoes and bring to the boil. Reduce the heat and leave it to simmer for 10 minutes, until rich and thick.

Meanwhile preheat your grill to high. When the tomato base is ready, pop your prawns in one layer into the sauce and crumble over the feta in medium-sized chunks. Place the frying pan under the grill for 6–8 minutes, until the prawns are cooked through and the feta starts to melt and turn golden. Remove the dish from the grill, sprinkle over the chopped parsley and serve straight away, with chunks of fresh bread to mop up the juices.

ADDICTIVE FENNEL CALAMARI: *KALAMARI ME MARATHOS*

Calamari doesn't really need much of an introduction, as it must be one of the most widely loved Mediterranean dishes. Good calamari is a great thing, however I'm sure we've all tried some that are below par, a little rubbery and chewy. Make sure to peel the squid as explained below and soak it before frying. I've included ground fennel seeds to my flour, which is a small step but one that really does make this popular snack all the more addictive.

SERVES 6–8

800g squid
75ml milk
1 litre vegetable oil
75g plain flour
sea salt and freshly ground
    white pepper
1 heaped teaspoon fennel seeds
a few fennel flowers, if available
lemons, to serve

This is an incredibly simple dish, but to get it right, and melt-in-the-mouth, you need to prepare it properly. Place the squid in a large bowl of cold water, and pull out the tentacles. Peel off the thin skin over the main cavity in the squid – it is thin and almost transparent. Discarding this will make the calamari more tender. Rinse them under running water a couple of times, washing the tentacles thoroughly to remove any sand. Cut the main body into rings, around 2cm wide. Drain the squid completely, then transfer to a large mixing bowl. Pour over the milk, toss to mix well, then cover the bowl and pop into the fridge for 30 minutes, to soften.

When the squid is ready, pour the oil into a large saucepan and place on a medium heat. In a large bowl mix the flour with a generous pinch of sea salt and a few good pinches of white pepper. Finely grind the fennel seeds and add to the flour. Drain the marinated squid and dry on kitchen paper, then transfer to the seasoned flour. Toss to coat all the squid pieces.

When the oil is ready (check by popping in a piece of bread or potato – it will turn golden when hot enough), remove the squid pieces from the flour, shaking off the excess, and fry for around 4–5 minutes, until golden and crisp. Don't overcrowd the pan, as it will cool the oil, so be sure to fry the calamari in batches. They will be pale for a while, and just when you think they aren't doing anything they turn golden – quickly spoon them out so they don't overcook.

Use a slotted spoon and transfer them to kitchen paper to drain off the excess oil. Serve straight away, sprinkled with a little extra salt, garnished with fennel flowers and with wedges of lemon on the side. Simple and perfect.

CYPRIOT PORK MEATBALLS: *KEFTEDES*

Growing up, if you asked me my favourite Greek food I would instantly respond with keftedes. These little deep-fried meatballs are insanely addictive, versatile and are/were always such a treat when one of my yiayias made them. Whether they are hot, straight from the pan, or cold the next day, I'm not fussy – they will be inhaled. As I grew older and travelled outside our little island, I realised that depending on where you went in Greece you would find different variations on keftedes or fritters. In Santorini, where they grow the sweetest cherry tomatoes, you find them made with these. In other parts of Greece they are made with courgettes, aubergines, greens and even chickpeas. Traditionally served as part of a meal or meze, they also make a great finger food or snack, with a yoghurt or dip on the side. Or you could eat them like we do, for dinner, with a huge chopped salad. Check out the vegetarian variations on page 103.

MAKES ABOUT 24

2 large potatoes, about 500–600g
1 onion
½ a bunch of flat-leaf parsley
500g pork mince
1 large egg
½ teaspoon baking powder
½ teaspoon ground cinnamon
½ teaspoon dried mint
¼ tsp white pepper
sea salt
100g fresh breadcrumbs
2 slices of white bread
1 litre vegetable oil

Peel the potatoes and coarsely grate them into a colander over a large mixing bowl. Squeeze the grated potato to get rid of the liquid and starch, then leave to one side while you get the rest of the ingredients ready, reserving the liquid in the bowl underneath.

Peel and finely chop the onion. Finely chop the parsley. Place both in a bowl with the mince, egg, baking powder, cinnamon, dried mint, white pepper and a generous few pinches of salt. Squeeze small handfuls of the grated potato to really extract all the moisture, and add to the pork mixture. Keep going until it is all used. (If you have had a bowl under the colander, gently discard the liquid and you'll see a starchy sediment at the bottom. Spoon this in also.) Really mix everything together well, and add 60g of the breadcrumbs. Bring it all together and see how it feels – this might be enough breadcrumbs, or you might feel like it needs a little more. Don't add too many, however, or it will dry out. Pat the mixture down, lay the slices of bread on top, and place the bowl in the fridge to rest for 1 hour. The bread will absorb any excess moisture.

When the mixture is ready, place the oil in a large saucepan and place on a medium heat. Cut a small cube of potato or bread and put into the oil. When it starts to sizzle and turn golden, the oil is ready to use. Use a tablespoon to scoop the mixture and with slightly wet hands mould into an oblong or round shape. Fry them in batches of 5 or 6, so the pan isn't overcrowded, for around 6–8 minutes, depending on their size. They should be golden and cooked through. Transfer to kitchen paper to drain off the excess oil, and keep going until all the mixture is used up. Serve straight away, or at room temperature. Delicious in all situations.

STUFFED VINE LEAVES AND OTHER VEG: *KOUPEPIA*

Considering they are potentially one of the most popular Greek, Turkish and Middle Eastern dishes, I rarely order or eat koupepia (aka koubebia/dolmades/dolma), as they tend to be a little too tough and not sweet enough. Reason being I've grown up eating them made by my Yiayia Maroulla, whose koupepia I consider to be the greatest. After she passed away I realised I never really ate them again. I watched her make them many times, but never properly wrote down the recipe. However, on my most recent trip to Cyprus three of her sisters each made them at different times and thankfully they were almost identical to my yiayia's. I have been able to piece the recipes together in order to share with you what I consider to be (almost) the best stuffed vine leaves out there. They won't be like the ones you buy in delis, they will be almost falling apart, so tender they melt in the mouth, and naturally sweet.

MAKES AROUND 45–50

2 onions
4 tablespoons olive oil
500g pork mince
sea salt
5 ripe tomatoes
2 tablespoons tomato purée
200g medium (or long) grain rice
1 tablespoon dried mint
½ teaspoon ground cinnamon
½ teaspoon freshly ground
   black pepper
½ a bunch of flat-leaf parsley
50 vine leaves (or you could try
   filling onions, courgettes, tomatoes
   and peppers)
800ml chicken stock
2 potatoes
2 lemons

Peel and finely chop the onions. Place the oil in a wide saucepan and soften the onions for 10 minutes, over a medium-low heat. Add the mince to the pan, turn it up a little and brown it so any water evaporates away. Season with salt and coarsely grate in 4 of the tomatoes, discarding the skins. Stir in the tomato purée and keep cooking until most of the juices have reduced, but you are left with a little liquid in the bottom of the pan. Stir in the rice, mint, cinnamon and black pepper. Season with salt. Finely chop the parsley and add to the pan. Leave to cool.

Blanch the vine leaves in boiling water for just a minute. To roll them, lay a leaf out in front of you, textured side up, with the stalk closest to you. Spoon a couple of teaspoons of the rice mixture towards the bottom of the leaf and roll it once, tuck in each side, then keep rolling until it has closed (the amount of mixture you use will depend on the size of the leaf – once you start you'll find your rhythm). Do this with all the leaves and filling.

Heat the chicken stock. Cut the potatoes into 1cm slices and line the bottom of a large saucepan with them. Layer up the koupepia so they are close together but not packed too tight (the rice will expand as it cooks). Coarsely grate the remaining tomato into the hot chicken stock, squeeze in the juice from the lemons, and pour over the layered vine leaves. If they are not quite covered with the liquid, add enough boiling water so they are just covered. Place an upturned heavy plate directly on top of the vine leaves, then cover the pan and place on a medium heat. Bring to a steady simmer, then reduce the heat and cook for 30 minutes, until most of the liquid has been absorbed and the koupepia are cooked through. Leave to rest for at least 15 minutes, covered, before serving.

3

VEGETABLES, GRAINS AND PULSES
—

YELLOW SPLIT PEA AND WILD FENNEL SOUP: *LOUVANA ME MARATHOS*

Louvana is so familiar, the kind of soup I have come across on my travels in many places. (Here in the UK we have pease pudding, for example, which isn't dissimilar.) However, to leave it out would be criminal, as it is a quintessential Cypriot recipe and eaten in abundance, especially around times of fasting. This is the classic recipe for louvana with the addition of wild fennel, one of my favourite springtime Greek ingredients. Also for an unorthodox addition, I occasionally top it with a poached egg, which works so well with the creamy soup. This, of course, is up to you, but I highly recommend it.

SERVES 6

1 onion
1 bulb of wild (or regular) fennel
2 leeks
300g yellow split peas
extra virgin olive oil
100g long-grain rice
sea salt and freshly ground
　black pepper
3 lemons
6 eggs (optional)

Peel and finely chop the onion. Trim and finely chop the fennel, reserving the fronds in a bowl of cold water for garnishing. Trim and finely slice the leeks. Place the yellow split peas in a sieve and wash them thoroughly under cold running water.

Place a large saucepan on a medium-low heat, drizzle in a few tablespoons of oil, and add the chopped veg (keeping back a little leek for garnishing, if you like). Sauté for 10 minutes until starting to soften. Stir in the washed yellow split peas and top with 1.6 litres of boiling water. Bring to the boil, then reduce to a simmer and cover with a lid. Simmer for 30 minutes, then stir in the rice (spooning off and discarding any scum that has come to the surface). Continue to cook for 30 minutes, or until everything is soft and creamy.

While the soup is cooking, sauté any reserved leeks in olive oil, for around 15 minutes or until golden. You can use this to garnish the soup. (This is not essential but adds an additional texture.) If you're poaching eggs, bring a pan of water to the boil.

When the soup is ready, blitz it a little with a stick blender if you like, adding a splash of boiling water if it has thickened too much. Finish by seasoning generously to taste and stirring in 3 tablespoons of extra virgin olive oil. Squeeze in the juice of 2 lemons, have a taste for balance, and cut the remaining lemon into wedges. Poach the eggs for 3 minutes. Serve bowls of the creamy, nourishing soup topped with a few caramelised leeks and reserved fennel fronds, an egg, and with the lemon wedges on the side.

Recipe overleaf

PUMPKIN, BULGUR WHEAT AND RAISIN PIE: *KOLOKYTHOPITA*

Kolokotes are small pasties filled with pumpkin, raisins and bulgur wheat, spiced with cinnamon – sweetly savoury little vegan snacks usually eaten around times of fasting. I thought of including the traditional recipe; however, I decided to give them a new lease of life as a wholesome yet fresh (and still vegan and Lent appropriate) pie – hopefully not upsetting too many yiayias in the process.
(Photo on previous page.)

SERVES 6

1kg pumpkin or butternut squash
2 red onions
1 teaspoon ground cinnamon
½ teaspoon ground allspice
olive oil
sea salt and freshly ground
   black pepper
50g bulgur wheat
1 lemon
1 tablespoon red wine vinegar
75g golden raisins
1 bunch of flat-leaf parsley
½ a bunch of coriander
1 × 270g pack of filo
   (for recipe, see page 265)
20g pumpkin seeds

Preheat the oven to 190°C/gas mark 5. Peel the pumpkin or butternut squash and cut into 4cm chunks, then spread out in a large roasting tray. Peel the onions, cut into thin wedges and add to the roasting tray, nestled between the squash chunks. Sprinkle over the ground cinnamon and allspice, drizzle with olive oil and season generously. Place in the oven and roast for 45 minutes, or until golden and cooked through. Remove from the oven and leave to cool a little.

Meanwhile put the bulgur wheat into a large bowl, season generously and cover with 300ml of boiling water. Cover with a lid or clingfilm, and leave to one side for 15 minutes. Drain in a sieve and leave to cool. Return to the bowl, squeeze over the juice of the lemon, stir in the vinegar and raisins and season.

Pick the parsley and coriander leaves and roughly chop. When the squash is ready, toss through the dressed bulgur wheat and add the chopped herbs. Give everything a taste, tweaking the seasoning.

Oil a 23cm loose-bottomed cake tin and layer over all but one sheet of filo, overlapping and brushing with oil as you go, making sure any excess hangs over the side. Fill the filo with the pumpkin mix and then place the remaining sheet over the top, doubling it up if possible. Brush with olive oil and fold over the filo draped over the edge. Scatter over the pumpkin seeds. Place on the bottom of the oven, reduce the heat to 180°C/gas mark 4, and bake for around 40 minutes, until golden and crisp all over. Remove from the oven, leave for 10 minutes in the tin, then carefully remove from the tin and serve.

TOMATO, AUBERGINE AND ROSEMARY SPAGHETTI

This is based on a recipe my mum still makes us. It's not an old-school Cypriot recipe, but a Socratous classic. It's perfect after-work food, and (as with most of our food) wonderful with a grating (or five) of halloumi over the top.

SERVES 4

4 garlic cloves
2 aubergines
olive oil
500g ripe tomatoes
6 sprigs of rosemary
12 black olives
¼ teaspoon chilli flakes
1 tablespoon red wine vinegar
sea salt and freshly ground
    black pepper
350g spaghetti (or pasta of
    your choice)

Peel and finely slice the garlic. Remove most of the aubergine skin (see page 13) and cut the flesh into 2–3cm pieces. Place a large saucepan on a medium heat and drizzle in a couple of tablespoons of olive oil. Fry the garlic for a minute or two until it starts to turn golden. Add the aubergines, season well and fry for about 15 minutes, until lightly golden all over. Meanwhile, chop the tomatoes, finely chop the rosemary leaves, and stone and tear the olives. Add them all to the pan, along with the chilli and vinegar, bring to the boil, then reduce the heat slightly so it bubbles away nicely for around 20 minutes. Stir occasionally to stop the sauce sticking. You want a thick, rich sauce, sweet and cooked down.

When the sauce is ready, bring a large pan of salted water to the boil. Cook the spaghetti according to packet instructions. When the pasta is ready, use a pair of tongs to drag it straight into the aubergine sauce. You want some pasta water in there too, to make it creamy and delicious. Toss all together and serve.

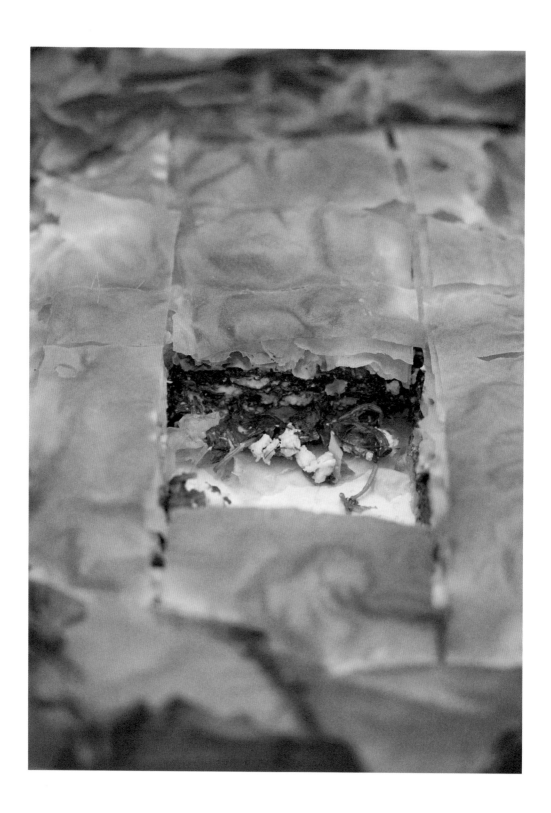

A VERY, VERY GOOD SPINACH AND FETA PIE: *SPANAKOPITA*

On a recent trip to my yiayia Martha's house I ate what can only be described as a life-changing spanakopita. That is a big claim, I'm aware, but I've eaten a lot of average and insipid spinach pies. I quizzed her and she said the key is not to wilt the greens first, as most people do, but to salt them to extract the moisture. This removes the water, but keeps the flavour – and you won't need to use kilos and kilos of spinach. I urge you to try it.

SERVES 8–12

800g spinach
6 spring onions
1 leek
1 tablespoon flaky sea salt
2 large eggs
200g feta
250g fresh anari or ricotta
80g rocket
½ teaspoon ground white pepper
nutmeg
1 bunch of dill
olive oil
270g filo (for recipe, see page 265)

You'll need a very large mixing bowl for this. Wash the spinach well. If using larger leaves, my yiayia says it needs to be washed at least three times to remove the dirt. Trim away any large stalks. Trim and finely slice the spring onions and leek. Rinse them in a colander to get rid of any dirt. Toss the spinach with the sliced veg (if your colander isn't large enough, do this in two stages). Sprinkle over the sea salt (or half of it if you are doing this in stages) and toss it in. Leave in the sink. After 15 minutes, use your hands to really scrunch the leaves, onions and leeks together, squeezing out the moisture. Be sure to really get stuck in and use your hands here, a spoon won't achieve the same thing. Once you have scrunched all the leaves, transfer them to your large mixing bowl, and repeat with the remaining ingredients if you are doing it in batches.

Preheat your oven to 190°C/gas mark 5. When the spinach is ready, whisk the eggs in a large mixing bowl. Crumble in the feta and fresh anari or ricotta (draining away any excess liquid from the ricotta) into the bowl. Add the rocket, ground white pepper and finely grate in a generous amount of nutmeg. Finely chop the dill, stalks and all, and mix it in.

Drizzle a little olive oil into a 25cm × 30cm roasting tray and, using a pastry brush, evenly coat the tray. Lay out enough filo to cover the base and drape over the sides, then drizzle with olive oil and brush it all over. Repeat until you have used half the filo; it should be around 3–4 (this will depend on the brand you use) layers thick. Spoon the spinach filling into the tray, spreading it out evenly, then top with the remaining filo so it is also around 4 layers thick, brushing each layer with olive oil as you go. Scrunch the overhanging filo around the edge of the pie and brush with olive oil. Gently score the top of the pie into 8–12 pieces, being careful not to cut all the way through. Place the tray in the oven, and bake for around 45 minutes, until golden all over, then remove and leave to rest for at least 30 minutes before serving.

LENTILS AND SPINACH WITH CRISPY SHALLOTS:
FAKI MOUTZENDRA ME SPANAKI

Faki is probably my most eaten Cypriot dish – what it lacks in looks it more than makes up for in flavour. It is one of the most comforting foods in my life, and would probably feature in my desert island dishes. We eat this with a huge chopped salad, which may sound odd to some as this is a warm dish, but it just works – a vinegary dressing cuts through the rich and earthy lentils beautifully.

SERVES 4

2 onions
2 garlic cloves
2 sticks of celery
olive oil
1 heaped tablespoon tomato purée
250g green lentils
1 bay leaf
80g long-grain rice
250g spinach
6 shallots
2 teaspoons cumin seeds
sea salt and freshly ground
    black pepper
a splash of red wine vinegar
Greek yoghurt, to serve

Peel and finely chop the onions and garlic, and finely chop the celery. Pour a couple of tablespoons of olive oil into a large saucepan and add all the chopped veg. Sauté on a low heat for 12–15 minutes, until soft and sticky but not coloured. Stir in the tomato purée, cook for a couple of minutes, then add the lentils and bay leaf. Stir everything together and pour over 1.5 litres of boiling water. Bring to the boil, then reduce the heat to low, cover with a lid and cook for 20 minutes, until the lentils are almost but not quite cooked. Stir in the rice, add a further 500ml of boiling water, so the lentils and rice are completely covered, and pop on the lid. Cook for 20 minutes.

Meanwhile, wash the spinach thoroughly and roughly chop it. Add it to the pan and cook for a further 10 minutes. You want the mixture to be slightly wet and oozy – the lentils and rice mixture shouldn't have absorbed all the water. If it has, be sure to add more.

Meanwhile, prepare the shallots. Peel and finely slice the shallots, into rings if possible. Place a large frying pan on a medium-low heat and pour in 3 tablespoons of olive oil. Add the cumin and fry for 30 seconds, then stir in the shallots. Sauté for 10 minutes, then turn up the heat a little so that the shallots become caramelised and slightly crisped, adding more oil if needed.

When the lentils are ready, season to taste and pour in 1 tablespoon of red wine vinegar – taste and add a little more if needed. Serve the lentils topped with the crispy shallots and with a generous helping of yoghurt and salad on the side.

ROASTED CAULIFLOWER IN SWEET TOMATO SAUCE: *KOUNOUPIDI YIAHNI*

My mum is the queen of this dish, and will still make it to entice us all home on a Sunday afternoon. Traditionally the cauliflower and potato would be fried before braising, but it is just as delicious roasted and a little kinder on the old ticker. Served with fresh sesame bread and pickles, it is perfect served from the pan at the table, and deceptively moreish. Also, much as you may want to eat this fresh, it is even more delicious the next day.

SERVES 4

1kg Cyprus potatoes, or other large
    waxy potatoes
extra virgin olive oil
sea salt and freshly ground
    black pepper
1 large head of cauliflower,
    or 2 regular sized ones
generous pinch of ground cinnamon
2 onions
2 garlic cloves
6 ripe tomatoes
1 tablespoon of tomato purée
2 bay leaves

Preheat your oven to 220°C/gas mark 7. Peel the potatoes and cut into 5cm chunks. Place them in a roasting tray, drizzle with a little oil and roast for 35 minutes, until they start to turn golden and are almost cooked through.

Meanwhile cut your cauliflower into large wedges, so that each piece is attached to the stalk still. Place in a large roasting tray and spread out in one layer. Season well and sprinkle over the ground cinnamon, then drizzle over a good glug of olive oil and rub in the seasoning. Roast for about 25 minutes, until cooked through and slightly charred. You want all the veg to have a nice bit of colour. When they are ready, remove from the oven and reduce the heat to 200°C/gas mark 6.

While the veg are cooking, get on with the sauce. Peel and finely chop the onions and garlic. Place a large ovenproof saucepan on a medium-low heat and drizzle in a couple of tablespoons of olive oil. Fry the garlic and onion for around 10 minutes, until soft and sticky. Peel the tomatoes (see page 12) and chop the flesh. Add the tomato purée to the pan, fry for a couple of minutes, then add the chopped skinned tomatoes, 300ml of boiling water, the bay leaves, and season well. Bring to the boil, then reduce the heat a little and cook for 10 minutes.

When the sauce and veg are all ready, finish the dish by layering the veg. Remove a little of the tomato sauce and set aside. Place the potatoes in the saucepan. Then put the cauliflower on top, sticking it upright if possible, so that the stalks are pointing down into the sauce. Spoon the reserved tomato sauce over the cauliflower and drizzle with a little olive oil. Place the pan in the oven and roast for 15–20 minutes, until the potato is perfectly cooked and the top is charred and gnarly. Serve with lots of fresh bread to mop up the juices and a bowl of your favourite pickles.

TOMATO BRAISED PEAS AND BEANS: *PIZELI KAI FASOLAKI YIAHNI*

I toyed with the idea of putting this in the sides section; however, it is more than filling enough to be a main meal (which is how we eat it), especially when served with all the traditional accompaniments. Like the roasted cauliflower on the previous page, we always have this with fresh Greek bread and pickled caper leaves, plus whole spring onions and a huge bowl of my mum's dressed tuna (page 131) – it's a perfect partnership. Also, I have called this 'pizeli and fazolaki yiahni' as we make it both ways, with peas or green beans, just use whichever you fancy.

SERVES 4

600g Maris Piper potatoes
olive oil
2 onions
3 carrots
5 ripe tomatoes or a 400g
    tin of tomatoes
1 tablespoon tomato purée
500ml vegetable stock
600g green beans or 900g fresh
    or frozen peas
4 large artichoke hearts

Peel the potatoes and cut into large chunks, around 5cm. Pour enough olive oil into a large saucepan to fill it by 1cm. Place on a medium heat and fry the potatoes on all sides until brown. Remove from the pan and keep to one side.

Meanwhile, peel and finely slice the onions. Peel and roughly chop the carrots. If using fresh tomatoes, peel them (see page 12), roughly chop and keep to one side. When the potatoes are done, fry the onions and carrots in the same pan for 10 minutes to soften slightly, reducing the heat a little. Stir in the tomato purée, then add the chopped or tinned tomatoes and the vegetable stock and bring to the boil. Reduce the heat and simmer for 15 minutes.

If using green beans, cut off the tops and roughly chop them in halves and thirds. Roughly chop the artichoke hearts. Stir the beans or peas and artichokes into the tomato sauce with the potatoes. Cover the pan and continue to cook for a further 35–40 minutes, or until the veg are soft and the sauce has thickened – you don't want it to be watery. Season to taste, and serve with all the accompaniments mentioned above.

Recipe overleaf

ROASTED CHICKPEA AND SESAME SOUP: *TAHINOSOUPA*

This soup fascinates me. I'd never heard of it before talking to my family about writing this book. This soup came about after a conversation with my uncle, who is now a priest in the Greek Orthodox church, and his stories of what the babas (priests) eat during times of fast. They eat Lenten foods for around a third of the year, hence why so many of our recipes are vegan and vegetarian. This recipe is so simple – and strangely addictive. I say strangely, because I am very aware that not everyone loves tahini. However, if you do, or if you are vegan, then I urge you to try it. I didn't want to play with it too much – the classic recipe doesn't have chickpeas in it, but they make a welcome addition, providing a rich nuttiness. Once you have made this, though, you can take it so many ways – it's a fantastic vehicle for other flavours and textures. (Photo on previous page.)

SERVES 6

2 × 400g tins of chickpeas
olive oil
sea salt and freshly ground
    black pepper
1 onion
1 carrot
1 stick of celery
125g long-grain rice or very
    small pasta (such as stars)
125g tahini
1–2 lemons
extra virgin olive oil

Preheat your oven to 190°C/gas mark 5. Drain one of the tins of chickpeas and spread out in a medium-sized roasting tray. Drizzle with olive oil, season generously and place in the oven for around 25 minutes, or until the chickpeas are golden all over.

Meanwhile, peel and finely chop the onion and carrot. Trim and finely chop the celery. Place a large saucepan on a medium-low heat and pour in a couple of tablespoons of olive oil. Add the veg and sauté for around 10 minutes so that they begin to soften. Stir in the rice, then after a minute add 750ml of boiling water and the remaining chickpeas, including the water in the tin. Turn the heat up to high, bring to the boil and season generously. Once boiling, reduce the heat to low, cover the pan and simmer gently for 15 minutes.

When the soup is ready, mix the tahini in a medium mixing bowl with 250ml of boiling water and the juice of 1 lemon. Pour the tahini mixture into the pan and stir into the soup. Gently heat through on a low heat for 3 minutes, until mixed together well. Use a stick blender to roughly blitz the soup. Check the seasoning, and add a little more lemon juice if needed. Serve drizzled with good extra virgin olive oil and scattered with the crispy chickpeas.

—

KEFTEDES AND CO, PART TWO:
AUBERGINE, TOMATO AND COURGETTE FRITTERS

If you have read the intro to the meat keftedes recipe (page 78), you'll know these little fritters are one of my favourite foods. In Cyprus you'll predominantly find them made with meat; however, in Greece, depending on where you visit, they can be made with a range of hero ingredients. Here are just three of them, with courgette probably the most popular. Aubergine is the most obscure, but it is a pleasant surprise, with an almost meaty texture and taste.

AUBERGINE KEFTEDES: *MELITZANOKEFTEDES*

MAKES 12–14

2 aubergines
1 onion
½ a bunch of flat-leaf parsley
50g kefalotyri or pecorino
1 teaspoon dried oregano
sea salt and freshly ground
    black pepper
1 large egg
100g self-raising flour
olive oil

Preheat your oven to 200°C/gas mark 6. Place the aubergines in a large roasting tray and cook for 1 hour, turning 3–4 times until charred, tender and cooked through. You can do this in advance and keep the aubergines in the fridge until you need them.

When you are ready to make the keftethes, peel and finely chop the onion. Finely chop the parsley. Place both in a large mixing bowl and scoop in the flesh of the cooked aubergines, discarding the skins. Finely grate in the cheese and mash everything together with a fork, breaking up the aubergine flesh as you go. Add the oregano, season generously and mix in the egg and self-raising flour. Pour a thin layer of oil in a large frying pan and place on a medium heat. Fry tablespoons of the mixture, for around 3 minutes on each side, until golden all over. Drain on kitchen paper, then serve straight away.

TOMATO KEFTEDES: *TOMATOKEFTEDES*

MAKES 16

500g ripe tomatoes
sea salt and freshly ground
  black pepper
½ a red onion
½ a bunch of basil
100g feta
125g self-raising flour
olive oil

Halve the tomatoes, then use a teaspoon to scoop out and discard the seeds. Finely chop the flesh, then place in a colander with ½ teaspoon of sea salt. Toss well and leave to drain over a bowl for half an hour.

When the tomatoes are ready, transfer them to a mixing bowl. Peel and finely chop the onion and pick and finely slice the basil leaves. Add to the tomatoes and crumble in the feta. Season with pepper and stir in enough flour to combine all the ingredients; you may not need all of it. Leave in the fridge for 30 minutes.

When you're ready to fry the keftedes, pour a thin layer of oil into a large frying pan and place on a medium heat. Fry tablespoons of the mixture for 4–5 minutes on each side, until golden all over. Drain on kitchen paper, then serve straight away – these ones really don't sit very well.

COURGETTE KEFTEDES: *KOLOKYTHOKEFTEDES*

MAKES 16

400g courgettes
4 spring onions
6 sprigs of mint
50g anari, salted ricotta or pecorino
½ a lemon
100g feta
sea salt and freshly ground
  black pepper
2 large eggs
125g self-raising flour
olive oil

Trim the courgettes and coarsely grate into a large mixing bowl. Trim and finely slice the spring onions. Pick and finely slice the mint leaves and add both to the courgettes. Finely grate in the anari and lemon zest and crumble in the feta. Whisk the eggs. Season, then add the eggs and whisk in along with the flour until everything just comes together.

Pour a thin layer of oil into a large non-stick pan, place on a medium-low heat and fry large tablespoons of the batter for around 4–5 minutes on each side until golden and cooked through. Drain on kitchen paper and serve, with the lemon half cut into wedges.

MY YIAYIA MAROULLA'S EGG AND CHIPS: *PATATES ME AVGA*

This might seem like a strange recipe to claim as Greek, but it is such a traditional dish. As you'll have seen in the Breakfast chapter (page 31), we Greeks and Cypriots love cooking anything we can in eggs. Whatever the time of year, we will use whatever is in season, from potatoes, like this recipe, or tomatoes, courgettes and artichokes, to more unusual ingredients such as mallow, amaranth and wild asparagus. Whenever I went to my Yiayia Maroulla's house she would always have a bowl of eggs and something seasonal cooked and ready to eat at all times.

There is so much flavour in this simple recipe, and unlike plain chips, it is still delicious when warm – it doesn't have to be eaten immediately.

SERVES 4

500g potatoes, Cyprus potatoes if you
    can get them, if not, Maris Pipers
1 onion
olive oil
1 litre vegetable oil
4 large eggs
sea salt and freshly ground
    black pepper
malt or white wine vinegar
sweet smoked paprika

Peel the potatoes, cut into slices, and then again into pieces around 2–3cm. Peel and finely slice the onion. Place a large frying pan on a medium-low heat and drizzle in a little olive oil. Add the onion and sauté for around 15 minutes, until softened, then turn up the heat a little for 5 more minutes, until a little golden and crisp around the edges.

Meanwhile, half fill a large saucepan with the vegetable oil, using less oil as needed as you don't want to overcrowd the pan. Place on a medium-high heat and pop a raw chip in there. When the chip is golden and has floated to the surface your oil is ready. Remove the chip and gently lower in the rest of them. Fry for around 10–15 minutes, or until they are golden and crisp (if your pan isn't very big you may need to do this in batches).

Meanwhile, whisk the eggs with a pinch of salt and pepper. When the chips are ready, use a slotted spoon to transfer them to a plate lined with kitchen paper to drain a little. Season with sea salt.

Transfer the chips to the pan with the onion and place on a high heat. Working quickly, pour in the eggs and scramble until everything is coated and glossy – try not to overcook the eggs. Finish with a little drizzle of vinegar and a sprinkle of paprika. Season to taste and serve.

STUFFED COURGETTE FLOWERS WITH MINT YOGHURT: *ANTHOUS ME GIAOURTI*

This is one of my favourite Cypriot summer dishes, and when I visit it's the first thing I ask my yiayia or aunties to make. Courgette flowers can be difficult to come by in the UK, but with so many people growing their own veg I thought it was worth including. Alternatively, ask a good greengrocer to source them for you. (If you are using your own, pick them in the morning when they have just opened and are at their most flavoursome, and before they fill with bugs – my yiayia's tip.)

SERVES 6

40 courgette flowers
3 ripe tomatoes
1 onion
½ a bunch of flat-leaf parsley
½ a bunch of mint
sea salt and freshly ground
    black pepper
a couple of pinches of ground
    cinnamon
350g medium or long-grain rice
2 medium courgettes
75ml olive oil
500g Greek yoghurt
1 lemon

Place the flowers in a large bowl of cold water, which will bring them back to life if they're a little wilted, and carefully remove the stamens inside (trying not to tear the petals).

Coarsely grate the tomatoes into a mixing bowl and discard the skins. Peel and finely chop the onion, then finely chop the parsley and half the mint leaves. Add the onion and herbs to the bowl of tomatoes. Season generously, add the cinnamon and stir in the rice. Use a teaspoon to gently fill each flower with the mixture, leaving a little overhang of the petals so they fold over on top to seal everything in as you twist them slightly.

Trim the courgettes and cut into ½cm slices. Drizzle half the olive oil into the base of a wide saucepan and lay the courgettes on the base in one layer (this is to stop the flowers sticking to the bottom and becoming damaged). Place the stuffed flowers on top, packing them in quite tightly, so they don't fall apart as they cook. Pour over 300ml of boiling water, or enough to cover the flowers by 1cm, season with salt and drizzle over the remaining olive oil. Cover the flowers directly with an upside-down plate. Place on the hob and simmer for around 20–25 minutes, or until the rice is completely cooked and most of the water has been absorbed. If they are not quite ready, add a splash more boiling water and cook for 5–10 more minutes. When ready, leave to cool slightly before serving.

While the flowers are cooking, prepare the yoghurt. Finely slice the remaining mint leaves and stir into the Greek yoghurt. Finely grate in the zest of the lemon and squeeze in the juice. Season well, and serve alongside the warm flowers.

CHEESE, COURGETTE AND HONEY PIE: *TYROPITA ME MELI*

Cheese pies are everywhere in Greece and Cyprus – small handheld ones and large sheet trays, in filo or kataifi, they take many guises. I am in love with this type, where you soak the cheese-filled pastry in a light custard and then bake it. It's such a simple and effective method that I've even developed a sweet pie made in a similar way, filled with apricots and pine nuts (page 233).

SERVES 6–8

large knob of butter
200g feta
175g kaseri or gruyère cheese,
   or even cheddar would work well
75g halloumi
350g courgettes
2 eggs
freshly ground white pepper
a few sprigs of thyme
300g kataifi pastry
175ml double cream
175ml milk
50g walnuts
olive oil
3 tablespoons honey

Grease a 25cm × 30cm roasting tray with the butter.

Crumble the feta into a bowl and coarsely grate in the other cheeses and the courgettes. Whisk one of the eggs, then add to the bowl along with a good pinch of white pepper. Pick in the thyme leaves and whisk it all together.

Tease the kataifi pastry apart and lay half of it in the greased tray, easing it up the sides a little. Fill with the cheese mixture, then drape over the remaining pastry until the filling is completely encased. Whisk together the remaining egg, cream and milk and pour evenly over the entire pie. Leave to one side for 30 minutes, preheating your oven to 180°C/gas mark 4 towards the end.

When you're ready to bake, finely chop the walnuts and scatter over the top of the pie. Drizzle everything with olive oil, then place directly on the bottom of the oven and bake for 35 minutes, until crisp and golden. Drizzle over the honey, return to the oven for 10–15 more minutes until dark golden, then leave in the tray for 10 minutes before serving.

YIAYIA MARTHA'S HALLOUMI AND MINT RAVIOLI: *RAVIOLES*

These are Cyprus's version of the more commonly known Italian ravioli. A proper housewife staple – as a family we all have a stash of these in our freezer. Yiayia loves to make them and we all love to eat them. Making the pasta here really isn't that tricky, and the filling is insanely easy. So once you get going, do as my yiayia does and make hundreds, and freeze them. When you are tired and hungry, you'll be so glad you did. If you're going to freeze them, make sure to do them in one layer on a tray, before putting them all into a bag. We store them layered in Tupperware, separated by greaseproof paper.

SERVES 4–6

500g village flour (see page 16),
　or tipo 00 pasta flour
60ml olive oil
2 × 250g blocks of halloumi
2 tablespoons dried mint
　(plus extra for serving)
½ a bunch of fresh mint
3 large eggs
a good pinch of black pepper
1.5 litres fresh chicken or
　vegetable stock
extra virgin olive oil
Halloumi, or salted anari
　or ricotta, to serve

To make the pasta dough, put the flour into a mixing bowl and rub in the olive oil until it resembles breadcrumbs. Add enough water to make a dough, around 75–100ml, and knead it on a clean surface until smooth and silky. This takes around 5 minutes. Wrap the dough in clingfilm and leave aside to rest for at least half an hour before using.

While the dough is resting, make the halloumi filling. Coarsely grate the halloumi into a mixing bowl and stir in the dried mint. Finely chop the fresh mint leaves and add to the bowl. Crack in 2 of the eggs and whisk into the mixture – it needs to be thick enough to fill the ravioles, not too wet. If it needs a little more binding however, add a bit more egg.

When the dough has rested, tear off small chunks and roll out on a pasta machine, working down the settings until it is quite thin but not too thin – the second or third setting from last. You can do this by hand with a long, thin rolling pin. The easiest way is to roll a sheet that is 7–8cm wide – the length doesn't matter too much as you will keep making more. Spoon teaspoonfuls of the mixture close to the bottom edge of the sheet, leaving a few centimetres between the spoonfuls. Lightly brush around the filling with a little water, then fold the top down, completely covering them. Use your fingers to press around the individual ravioles, sealing the filling in completely. Use a 5cm glass to cut the ravioles into half moons, or use a ravioli cutter, if you wish. Place the finished ones on a flour-dusted tray as you go.

When you're ready to cook the ravioles, bring the stock to the boil in a large saucepan and drizzle in a little olive oil. Cook the ravioles for around 10–12 minutes, pushing them down every so often with a slotted spoon as they float to the surface. Serve in deep bowls, with a ladleful of the hot stock, drizzled with a little extra virgin olive oil. Finish with a grating of halloumi or anari, to be super indulgent, and a sprinkle of dried mint.

Recipe overleaf

CREAMY CHICKPEAS AND CHARD: *REVITHIA ME LAHANA*

Yiayia Maroulla made the most melt-in-the-mouth chickpeas, and her secret was a pressure cooker. They really do work wonders with dried pulses, making them more tender than you could ever achieve cooking with tinned ones. Most people don't own a pressure cooker nowadays (and releasing the steam always slightly terrified me), and although I do make an effort to cook my own chickpeas, I will sometimes buy the jarred variety. They are more expensive, but I enjoy them so much more than tinned that I feel like they are worth it. (Photo on previous page.)

SERVES 4

300g dried chickpeas or a 600g
   jar or good-quality tinned
3 teaspoons of bicarbonate of soda
   (if using dried chickpeas)
4 sticks of celery
500g Swiss chard or cavolo nero
3 tablespoons olive oil
6 anchovies
¼ teaspoon dried chilli
8 sprigs of fresh oregano
   (or ½ teaspoon dried)
1 lemon
freshly ground black pepper

If cooking your own chickpeas, start the day before (see page 16 for advice).

Trim and finely slice the celery. Wash the chard or cavolo nero – if using cavolo nero, remove and discard the stalks. If using chard, finely slice the stalks. Keep the leaves to one side. Place a wide saucepan on a medium-low heat and drizzle in the olive oil. Sauté the celery and chard stalks for 10 minutes until they start to soften. Add the anchovies, chilli and oregano leaves and fry for a few minutes, so that the anchovies dissolve. Tear in the chard or cavolo nero leaves to the pan, stir, then cover with a lid for 10 minutes to soften. Remove the lid and stir in the drained chickpeas, plus a mug of the cooking liquor or the liquid from the jar. Cover with the lid and cook for 10 more minutes, until everything is hot and any liquid is a little creamy. Squeeze in the juice of the lemon and season generously with black pepper. Delicious served hot, or even at room temperature.

CLASSIC BAKED BEANS: *GIGANTES*

An absolutely classic recipe. Think of these as giant, more flavoursome baked beans – without the tonne of added sugar. And you can happily embellish them if you wish: fry sliced streaky bacon or add broken up sausages to the base. Or garnish with broken-up feta before baking. Delicious. (Photo on page 66.)

SERVES 8

500g dried gigantes beans
2 garlic cloves
1 red onion
2 carrots
2 stick of celery
olive oil
1 teaspoon dried oregano
1 tablespoon tomato purée
1 × 400g tin of tomatoes
1 stick of cinnamon
sea salt and freshly ground
   black pepper

Start the night before by soaking the beans in plenty of water. You'll need to soak them for at least 12 hours.

When you are ready to cook the beans, place a large saucepan of water on to boil. Drain the soaked beans and place most of them in the boiling water. Reserve a handful and peel off the white skin (if possible, some will come off easier than others). I like to do this with a handful of the beans so that they disintegrate into the stew and make it thick and creamy. Once peeled, add them to the pan and simmer for 45 minutes.

Meanwhile peel and finely chop the garlic. Peel and roughly chop the onion and carrots. Trim and slice the celery. Place a large casserole pan on a medium-low heat and pour in 3 tablespoons of olive oil, then add all the chopped veg. Start to soften for 10 minutes, then stir in the oregano and tomato purée. Fry for a minute, then add the tinned tomatoes, cinnamon stick and 400ml of water. Bring to the boil, then simmer on a low heat for 5 minutes. Season generously. Preheat your oven to 180°C/gas mark 4.

When the beans have finished their 45 minutes, spoon them into the tomato sauce with a slotted spoon. I do this, rather than drain them completely, as you want a little of the cooking water in there (reserve a mug of the cooking water for later on, too). Give them a good stir, cover with the lid and place in the oven for 45 minutes. When that time's up, remove them from the oven, stir in a splash of the reserved cooking water and return to the oven, uncovered, for 15 minutes. Remove from the oven, stir in the rest of the water, add a good drizzle of olive oil and pop back for a final 15 minutes. Remove from the oven, leave to rest, and serve warm.

SLOW-COOKED GARDEN BEANS WITH SAUSAGE: *FASOLIA ME LOUKANIKO*

You'll have realised we eat a lot of pulses in Cyprus. They're inexpensive, incredibly good for you and are good for Lenten meals. I've added sausage here, but really it could also be a vegan dish. I've named this dish 'garden beans' because of the vast amount of veg in it, and it isn't a strict recipe – if you have chard or marrow/courgettes, feel free to add them at the end. Anything that makes it sweeter is welcome. And much as I like to cook my own beans, I know there isn't always time, so feel free to use tinned or jarred beans instead, for a quicker recipe.

SERVES 6–8

500g dried white beans, such as
    white kidney beans or cannellini,
    or 3 × 400g tins or 2 × 600g jars
3 tablespoons olive oil
4 loukaniko sausages or
    spicy sausages (optional)
2 onions
3 carrots
1 large potato, around 325g
4 sticks of celery
4 ripe tomatoes
1 tablespoon tomato purée
1 litre of vegetable stock
2 bay leaves
sea salt and freshly ground
    black pepper
extra virgin olive oil

If using dried beans, place them in a large mixing bowl and cover with plenty of water. Soak overnight. If using jarred or tinned beans follow the instructions below but use a half quantity of vegetable stock.

The next day place a large saucepan on a medium-low heat and pour in the olive oil. Roughly chop the loukaniko, if using, and add to the pan. If using a traditional sausage, squeeze the meat from the skins into the pan, and discard the skins. Fry for around 8–10 minutes, until lightly browned.

While the sausage is frying, peel and finely chop the onions. Peel the carrots and slice into 1cm pieces, and peel the potato and chop into 3cm chunks. Trim the celery and cut the same size as the carrot. Chop the tomatoes. Add the onion, carrot and celery to the fried sausage meat and sauté for 10 minutes. Stir in the tomato purée, then add the chopped tomatoes and vegetable stock and bring to the boil. Add the bay leaves, potatoes and drained beans. Stir everything together, then cover and reduce the heat to low. Cook for 1 hour and stir occasionally. If it looks like it is getting a little dry, be sure to add a splash of boiling water. If using any other veg, such as chard or courgettes, wash and roughly chop and add for the last 20 minutes of cooking.

After an hour, remove the lid, make sure everything is cooked through and cook on a slightly higher heat for 15 minutes to reduce and thicken. Season generously and serve drizzled with extra virgin olive oil and with good bread.

FRESH BLACK-EYED BEANS AND MARROW: *LOUVI FRESKO ME TO KOLOKOUI*

When I was discussing this book with family members, one recipe that kept coming up was louvi me to kolokoui. It is one of my favourite Cypriot meals. In an age when we are able to get almost any ingredient at any time of year, part of the beauty and appeal of this dish is the wait. We wait ten months of the year for the summer, when fresh black-eyed beans and a specific type of courgette/marrow are in season. We hound the local Cypriot grocers to find out when both will be brought in, then buy it in bulk and gorge on it for the very few days or (hopefully) weeks that it is available. By the end of August, the time is up and it is back to waiting again. Is it the best dish in the world? Probably not for most people, but for Cypriots it is heaven, heightened by anticipation. To feature a recipe for it is a little mad though, as most people won't be able to get the ingredients, and really it isn't much of a recipe.
But it's important, so I wanted to give it the nod it deserves.

To cook, trim the fresh black-eyed beans, and remove any long fibres. Cut the smaller pods in half or thirds. For any larger pods, remove the beans and discard the casing. Half fill a large saucepan with water, bring to the boil and add the prepared beans and pods. Cook for 20 minutes while you prepare the kolokoui, skimming away any scum that rises to the surface. Trim the courgette/marrow and cut into large chunks, around 5cm, and scoop out the seeds as you go. After 20 minutes, add the prepared kolokoui to the pan, reduce the heat, cover the pan and simmer for a further 10–15 minutes until everything is tender. Discard most of the cooking water, leaving around 4cm in the bottom of the pan for serving.

To serve, ladle the veg into bowls with a little of the reserved cooking liquor. Drizzle with a generous pouring of good extra virgin olive oil, lots of fresh lemon juice and season well. Eat it with fresh koulouri and my mum's dressed tuna (see page 131).

4

FISH
—

CHARGRILLED SQUID WITH CHILLI AND OREGANO:
KALAMARI STA KARVOUNA

I adore this simple, surprisingly moreish recipe. It's perfect as part of a meze, served with salad, or even, just as a light snack with a glass of good wine.

SERVES 4–6

600g squid, cleaned
2 tablespoons ouzo
olive oil
½ teaspoon dried red chilli
1 teaspoon dried oregano
3 garlic cloves
sea salt and freshly ground
    black pepper
1–2 lemons

Place the squid on a large chopping board and pull out the tentacles. Cut the tubes open and peel off the thin membrane that is over the main body – it is thin and almost transparent. Discarding this will help make the squid tender. Rinse everything under running water a couple of times, washing the tentacles thoroughly to remove any grit. Using a sharp knife, score the main body in a criss-cross pattern, being careful not to cut it all the way through, then cut into 4cm pieces. Place all the squid in a large mixing bowl, then sprinkle over the ouzo, a good glug of olive oil and the dried chilli and oregano. Crush the garlic cloves with the side of your knife and add to the bowl. Toss to combine, cover the bowl and leave in the fridge overnight to marinate.

When you are ready to cook the squid, preheat your griddle pan on a high heat or, even better, get your barbecue ready. Griddled the marinated squid pieces for a couple of minutes on each side, until cooked through and nicely charred. Season generously and serve straight away, with lemons cut into wedges.

FISH KEFTEDES IN MUSTARD AND DILL

Not an authentic keftedes recipe, but (a hugely popular) one I developed for my half pescatarian family. It combines the Greek love of fritters and meatballs with mustard sauce – a common addition to souvlakia or gyro.

SERVES 4

½ teaspoon fennel seeds
½ a bunch of flat-leaf parsley
100g fresh breadcrumbs
600g white fish fillets – such as
   cod, haddock or pollock –
   skinless and boneless
2 large eggs
sea salt and freshly ground
   black pepper
olive oil
4 spring onions
2 garlic cloves
2 teaspoons French mustard
400ml crème fraîche
1 tablespoon capers
½ a bunch of dill

Preheat your oven to 200°C/gas mark 6. Grind the fennel seeds in a pestle and mortar, then transfer to a food processor. Roughly chop the parsley and add to the processor along with the breadcrumbs, then pulse once. Cut the fish into small chunks, add and blitz until just blended together. Crack in the eggs, season well and pulse once or twice, till everything is just combined. Roll the mixture until small balls, around 3–4cm. Drizzle a few tablespoons of olive oil into a large ovenproof frying pan and place on a medium heat. Fry the fish balls on all sides until golden brown and crisp all over, then spoon onto a plate.

Trim and finely slice the spring onions, peel and finely chop the garlic. Drizzle a little more olive oil into the pan and sauté the spring onions and garlic for 10 minutes on a low heat, then stir in the mustard and crème fraîche. Heat for a couple of minutes, then season and pop the fish balls back in. Scatter over the capers and transfer the pan to the oven. Bake for 10 minutes. Finely chop the dill, scatter over the dish and serve. Perfect with a stack of pita breads and a big chopped salad.

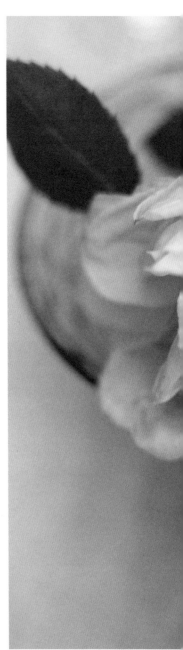

Recipe overleaf

GARLIC BUTTER PRAWNS WITH ORZO: *KRITHARAKI ME GARIDES*

This is my mum's interpretation of kritharaki in which she substitutes the more commonly used chicken (see page 162) with prawns, so that my pescatarian dad can still enjoy it. It is quick but feels indulgent and makes a fabulous after-work meal.

SERVES 2

4 stalks of chard
2 onions
3 garlic cloves
olive oil
100g orzo
400g ripe tomatoes
150ml white wine
500g vegetable stock
40g butter
12 king prawns, butterflied
a few pinches of dried red chilli
½ a lemon

Remove the chard stalks from the leaves. Finely slice the stalks and roughly slice the leaves. Peel and finely chop the onions and 1 garlic clove. In a medium saucepan, add a good glug of olive oil and the onion, garlic and chard stalks. Sauté over a medium-low heat for 10 minutes. Stir in the orzo for 1 minute, then grate in the tomatoes, discarding the skins, and add the wine. Bring to the boil and bubble away until reduced by half. Heat the stock, then stir in, season well, and bring to the boil. Reduce the heat to low and simmer for 10 minutes, then stir in the chard leaves. Cover and simmer for a further 10 minutes, until cooked through and creamy, adding a splash of water if it looks a little dry.

When the orzo is almost ready, peel and finely slice the remaining 2 garlic cloves. Melt the butter in a frying pan with a drizzle of olive oil and fry the garlic over a medium heat for a minute, then add the prawns and dried chilli. Fry for 4–5 minutes, until the prawns are cooked through and a little golden. Serve the oozy orzo topped with the buttery prawns and a wedge of lemon.

MAMA'S DRESSED TUNA

I didn't know if this recipe was authentic, only that my mum and Yiayia Maroulla would always make it alongside any of the hearty traditional vegan and veggie dishes. Its appearance with dishes like pizeli and fasolaki yiahni (page 98) and louvi fresko me to kolokoui (page 121) make them a real feast. Then, through the joys of social media, I found out that it's a staple in many Greek Cypriot households, making it more than just a Socratous or Panayiotou family recipe.

For so many years I tried to recreate this just as my mum and yiayia made it and couldn't get it right. I knew the ingredients, Mum had told me, so what was wrong? I only found out when writing this book. I was using tuna in brine; quizzing my mum revealed it has to be tuna in oil. Lo and behold, it made all the difference. (Photo on page 99.)

SERVES 4–6

2 × 200g tins of tuna in oil
1 bunch of spring onions
1 bunch of coriander
2 lemons
extra virgin olive oil
sea salt and freshly ground
    black pepper

Drain the tuna and flake into a mixing bowl. Trim and finely slice the spring onions and finely chop the coriander, stalks and all. Add both to the tuna and squeeze in the juice of the lemons. Drizzle over a few good glugs of olive oil and season generously. Stir together and refrigerate till needed.

POMEGRANATE AND THYME SWORDFISH SOUVLAKI: *SOUVLAKI XIFIAS ME RODI*

Even though souvla and souvlaki are traditionally made with meat (see page 148), you'll now find fish and vegetarian options in many places. Due to there being so many pescatarians in my family we always have fish options on the barbecue, and swordfish is the most popular. Its meaty texture makes it a perfect seafood skewer option.

MAKES 4 SKEWERS

2 shallots
3 garlic cloves
2 tablespoons olive oil
1 tablespoon pomegranate molasses, plus extra for finishing
½ teaspoon dried thyme
600g swordfish fillet
1 bulb of fennel
1 cucumber
a few sprigs of mint
300g Greek yoghurt
sea salt and freshly ground black pepper
2 tablespoons pomegranate seeds
4 pita breads
1 lemon

Peel and roughly chop the shallots and 2 of the garlic cloves. Place in a mini chopper with the olive oil, pomegranate molasses and dried thyme and blitz to a paste. Cut the swordfish into even chunks, about 3cm, and place in a mixing bowl with the marinade. Mix together well, cover and leave in the fridge until needed. If you can, do this the day before, but even a few hours in the fridge is great.

Get your BBQ ready, or preheat a griddle pan. Before you are ready to cook your souvlaki, make the accompaniments. Trim and shave the fennel and cucumber. Pick in the mint leaves and leave to one side. Finely grate or crush the remaining garlic into the yoghurt, season well and stir together.

Thread the swordfish onto skewers – don't pack them too close together or they won't cook evenly. Griddle them on all sides for a couple of minutes, seasoning as you go, until charred and just cooked through. Warm some pita bread at the same time. Split the pita and spoon the garlic yoghurt inside, then top with the hot swordfish souvlaki. Drizzle over a little pomegranate molasses and scatter over the pomegranate seeds. Squeeze the lemon over the fennel salad and serve on top of the fish.

VINE ROASTED BREAM: *TSIPOURAS SE KLIMATOFILA*

This simple recipe takes minutes to prepare. Vine leaves make an interesting and elegant casing for the fish, protecting the marinade and keeping the fish moist. However, if you can't find them, don't worry, use greaseproof paper. Just be sure to dampen it under running water first and give it a good squeeze.

SERVES 2

2 garlic cloves
8 green olives
½ teaspoon coriander seeds
1 bunch of coriander
4 anchovies
olive oil
1 lemon
sea salt and freshly ground
   black pepper
2 whole sea bream or bass,
   around 300g each
12 vine leaves

Preheat your oven to 200°C/gas mark 6. Peel the garlic cloves. Remove the stones from the olives. Blitz both in a food processor along with the coriander seeds, fresh coriander, anchovies and garlic, adding just enough olive oil to make it into a paste. Finely grate in the lemon zest and season well.

Score one of the fish 3 times on each side and rub half of the marinade all over the fish. Lay out 4 vine leaves, overlapping slightly, and place the sea bream on top. Finely slice the lemon and place half the slices in the cavity. Fold the leaves over the fish, top with 2 more leaves to make sure it is completely covered, then gently tie the whole thing together with string to keep it sealed. (Don't worry if it doesn't look perfect.) Place in a large roasting tray, then repeat with the remaining ingredients. Drizzle everything with olive oil and place in the oven. Roast for 15–20 minutes, until browned and crisp, and the fish is cooked through. To check, carefully open a package near the head and insert a skewer into the thickest piece of the flesh. Leave it there for a few seconds, then touch the tip of the skewer to your lips – carefully. It should be piping hot, and if it is that means the fish is cooked through. Cut and remove the strings, then place the vine-leaf parcels on plates to open at the table. Serve with Cypriot potato salad (page 210) or krambosalata (page 192) for a fresh, coast-worthy meal.

SEAFOOD AND SAFFRON PILAFI: *PILAFI RISI ME THALASSINA*

Pilafi is usually an accompaniment to main dishes; however, this risotto-like dish lends itself to being embellished and served as a main. We love the addition of seafood, and always serve it with a large tub of the creamiest, tangiest Greek Cypriot yoghurt (eaten at an almost 50:50 ratio).

SERVES 4

2 onions
2 garlic cloves
2 sticks of celery
olive oil
75g butter
80g vermicelli
350g ripe tomatoes
250g long-grain rice
800ml fish stock
a good pinch of saffron
1 stick of cinnamon
75g golden raisins
500g seafood – squid rings,
    prawns, mussels
½ teaspoon dried chilli
60g pine nuts
½ a bunch of flat-leaf parsley
sea salt and freshly ground
    black pepper
1 lemon

Peel and finely slice the onions and garlic. Trim and finely slice the celery, set aside. Place a large saucepan on a medium heat, then drizzle in a good swig of olive oil and add a tablespoon of the butter. Crush the vermicelli into small pieces and fry until golden and crisp. Spoon into a bowl and leave to one side. Lower the heat a little and add the sliced veg to the pan. Sauté for 15 minutes, or until golden and sticky. Finely chop the tomatoes, add to the saucepan along with the rice, and stir for a couple of minutes.

Heat the stock, then add the saffron and leave for a few minutes. Pour into the saucepan along with the cinnamon, golden raisins and the crisp vermicelli. Bring to the boil, then reduce to low and cover with a lid. Cook for 15 minutes.

While the rice is cooking, prepare the seafood. Clean the shellfish, discarding any that don't close (see page 15). Remove any veins from the prawns. When the rice's 15 minutes are up, stir in the seafood, add a splash of boiling water if the rice is looking dry and cover with a lid again. Cook for a further 5 minutes, until the shellfish is cooked (discarding any mussels that haven't opened) and the liquid has been absorbed.

Meanwhile melt the remaining butter in a small pan over a medium heat. Add the dried chilli and pine nuts and toast until the pine nuts are golden. Chop the parsley and stir through the pilafi when it is cooked. Season the pilafi to taste, drizzle with the spicy pine nut butter and serve with the lemon, cut into wedges.

BARBECUED RED-WINE BRAISED OCTOPUS: *CHTAPODI STA KARVOUNA*

One of my most memorable food moments is being on an uninhabited island in Greece, cooking octopus on a fire I made in the ground. I braised it first in red wine, then finished it over my small fire. The octopus was fresh, the sun was shining, the sea was less than ten metres away.

Surely one of the most quintessential Greek images is of octopuses hanging on a line, drying and tenderising in the sunshine. It's a method still used – you see it everywhere in Greece and Cyprus. Once they've caught an octopus, the fishermen will beat it on rocks to tenderise it and break down the fibres, then hang it up before cooking. You don't need to go to that extent to cook your octopus; it's actually much simpler than most people realise. Just get your fishmonger to prep it first and remove the ink sac. Frozen octopus is often already prepared; you just have to remove the beak, but you can always cut it out after cooking.

SERVES 4

2 onions
olive oil
½ a bottle of red wine
2 bay leaves
½ teaspoon black peppercorns
1 tablespoon red wine vinegar
1 octopus, around 1kg, cleaned
   by your fishmonger
1 lemon
½ teaspoon dried oregano

Peel and roughly chop the onions. Place a large saucepan on a medium-low heat, drizzle in a few tablespoons of olive oil and sauté the onions for 10 minutes, until they start to soften. Add the red wine, bay leaves, peppercorns and red wine vinegar to the pan and turn the heat up (don't add any salt, as the octopus is salty enough). Bring to the boil, lower in the octopus, then cover the pan and lower to a simmer. Cook for about 1 hour, or until the octopus is tender – a sharp knife should go into the thickest part of the tentacle easily. If not, cover and continue to cook, checking at 10-minute intervals. Be careful not to overcook it, or it'll dry out.

Meanwhile, light your barbecue. Squeeze the lemon juice into a bowl, top with the same amount of olive oil and whisk in the dried oregano. When the octopus is ready, remove from the pot and cut into large pieces (or you can do this after barbecuing, whichever you prefer). Barbecue the octopus pieces until nicely charred all over, basting with the lemon dressing as you go. As it is already perfectly cooked, the octopus doesn't need long, just enough time to char all over and add flavour. Serve immediately.

SPICY TOMATO MUSSELS WITH FETA: *MYDIA SAGANAKI*

This recipe is from my dear cousin Cassie, who loves food as much as I do and spends her summers eating her way around Greece. There, many recipes are called 'saganaki', referring to the vessel they're cooked in – a wide, two-handled shallow pan. Mussels are often cooked in this kind of pan, just like the prawn saganaki in the meze chapter (page 74). However, making it for a meze usually involves removing the mussels from their shells, and to be honest I prefer it as a larger portion. So, for familiarity purposes, I am keeping the name but making this more of a meal. With a glass of chilled wine and a big piece of crusty bread it is superb.

SERVES 2

500g fresh mussels, cleaned
300g ripe tomatoes
2 garlic cloves
1 red chilli
olive oil
½ tablespoon tomato purée
1 teaspoon dried oregano
200ml white wine
freshly ground black pepper
60g feta
a few sprigs of parsley
a few sprigs of dill

Prepare the mussels first by rinsing them under cold water. If any are broken or don't shut when you gently tap them it means they're dead, so discard them (see page 15 for tips). Pull any beards off of the shut mussels. Leave them in the fridge until you are ready to cook them.

Finely chop the tomatoes and keep to one side. Peel and finely slice the garlic. Halve, deseed and finely slice the chilli. Place a pot large enough to hold all the mussels on a medium-low heat and drizzle in a few table-spoons of olive oil. Add the garlic and chilli and fry for a minute or two until lightly golden. Stir in the tomato purée, oregano and the chopped tomatoes and fry for 10 minutes, until soft and sticky. Add the white wine and bring to the boil, then reduce slightly and leave to simmer for 10 minutes, until it has almost cooked away. Add the prepared mussels, cover with a lid and leave to cook for 5 minutes, until they have all opened. Discard any that don't open at all. Finish with a good pinch of pepper and crumble over the feta. Finely chop the herbs, scatter over and serve straight away.

TUNA, BABY ONION AND RED WINE STEW: *TONO STIFADO*

This recipe comes from my friend Andy, who spends a lot of time on the Greek islands and loves to spearfish. I was lucky enough to travel around Greece with him, and saw him catch a large tuna which we cooked on a barbecue. Greeks rarely do much to fish, preferring to cook it simply over fire with lots of lemon and oil; however, if you want to try your hand at something a little more involved, this meaty and rich stifado is a winner.

SERVES 6

600g baby onions
75ml olive oil
1 red onion
3 garlic cloves
1 tablespoon dried oregano
2 bay leaves
1½ tablespoons tomato purée
400g plum tomatoes (or a 400g
  tin of plum tomatoes)
sea salt and freshly ground
  black pepper
1 stick of cinnamon
5 whole cloves
½ tablespoon ground allspice
2 tbsp red wine vinegar
250ml red wine
1kg piece of tuna
½ a bunch of flat-leaf parsley

Peel the baby onions, leaving them whole. You can make this easier by covering them with boiling water for a few minutes first. Heat half the olive oil in a large saucepan over a medium heat and sauté the baby onions for 8–10 minutes until they start to soften, stirring occasionally. Transfer to a bowl.

Peel and finely slice the red onion and garlic. Add them to the pan along with the oregano and bay leaves and sauté for 5 minutes until softened. Stir in the tomato purée, coarsely grate in the plum tomatoes, season generously with salt and pepper, and cook for 10 minutes over a low heat. Add the cinnamon, cloves, allspice, red wine vinegar, red wine and baby onions and bring to the boil. Reduce the heat and continue to cook for 10 minutes.

Meanwhile, cut the tuna into 4–5cm chunks. Heat the remaining oil in a large frying pan over medium heat and sear the tuna chunks for a few minutes on each side. Transfer carefully into the tomato sauce, then stir the mixture gently. Continue to cook over a low heat for 20–30 minutes, or until the sauce has thickened. Finely chop the parsley and sprinkle over the finished stifado. Serve with some bread or rice to mop up the sauce.

FISHERMAN'S STEW: *KAKAVIA*

Kakavia is a hearty, one-pot meal, and a great way to use whatever seafood is fresh and in abundance. You can even add shellfish towards the end – prawns, mussels and clams would all make fine additions. Like with most stews and one-pot dishes, it is delicious fresh, but even more so the next day.

SERVES 4

1 onion
2 carrots
4 sticks of celery
1 leek
2 garlic cloves
olive oil
400g ripe tomatoes
600g Cyprus potatoes
2 bay leaves
3 allspice berries
1 litre of fish or shellfish stock
sea salt and freshly ground
  black pepper
750 fish fillets, such as hake,
  sea bass, bream, red mullet, etc.,
  scaled and pin-boned
1 lemon
1 bunch of dill or flat leaf parsley

Peel and chop the onion and carrots. Trim and slice the celery and leek. Peel and finely chop the garlic. Place a large saucepan on a medium heat and drizzle in a few tablespoons of olive oil. Sauté the veg for 15–20 minutes, until starting to soften but not golden.

Cut the tomatoes into 3cm pieces and add to the pan. Sauté for a few minutes. Scrub the potatoes, then chop into the same size as the tomatoes and add along with the bay leaves, allspice and stock. Season well, bring to the boil, then cover and reduce to a simmer for 25 minutes. Cut the fish into even-sized chunks, around 4–5cm, and add to the pan. Simmer for 10 minutes, until the fish is just cooked through. Squeeze in the juice of the lemon. Finely chop the dill and add to the pan, then serve.

5

MEAT

—

SOUVLA, SOUVLAKIA AND SHEFTALIA

Greeks and Cypriots are hugely passionate about meat over fire. Not just any old barbecue – the contraption you will find in almost every Greek home is called a foukou and it is a thing to behold. It is a long rectangular barbecue with grooves for big skewers to sit lengthways, grooves widthways for short skewers, and motors to turn them both in opposite directions, rotisserie style. It doesn't matter what the weather, we take it very seriously. I currently live in a largely Cypriot populated area of London, and on any given Sunday, rain or shine, you can walk the streets and be greeted by the smell of souvla.

So what is the difference between souvla, souvlakia and sheftalia?

Souvla means 'skewer' and is a dish most commonly cooked in Cyprus. We use large, thick skewers, and cook fist-sized chunks of pork, lamb or even chicken very slowly over white coals. A proper souvla will take anywhere between 1½ and 3 hours to cook, as we use fattier cuts of meat such as neck and shoulder, and the skewers shouldn't be too close to the heat. You'll find souvla eaten whenever nowadays, but historically it was saved for special occasions and celebrations.

Souvlakia (the diminutive of souvla) is found in both Greece and Cyprus but is served differently in each country. It is fast food, hand held and most commonly made with pork and chicken cut into small cubes, cooked on small skewers. If you are ordering in Greece, the term changes depending where you are: order souvlaki in the north and you will receive the pork skewers straight up. In Athens and the south, you will receive the skewers enveloped in a round, slightly fluffy pita bread with all the trimmings – tomato, tzatziki or a mustard sauce, chips, onions, etc. For just the meat skewers you would need to order a 'kalamaki' which means reed (my cousin Cassie informs me if you order a kalamaki in the north you will be given a straw as a joke).

In Cyprus, souvlaki can be either the skewer or the finished dish. It can be served as a meal but mostly it comes in a pita. Cypriot pita is oval, less fluffy, with a pocket style opening and filled to the brim with tomato, cucumber, shredded cabbage, onion and parsley. It is lighter than the Greek version. You will often find pickled green chillies in there and there will always be lemon wedges.

(Just to confuse you even more there is gyro. Gyro means 'to turn', and unfortunately has been given bad rep by thousands of dodgy kebab houses. We've all seen those elephant legs in the kebab shop windows, and they are pretty gutting, because a good version of a gyro is a great thing. It is a large spear piled high with chunks of meat, fat and flavourings – oregano, paprika, garlic– rotating next to a vertical grill. The meat on the outside is 'shaved' off into a pita bread and then it is finished with the regular trimmings.)

Finally, there are sheftalia. A traditional Cypriot recipe, sheftalia are like small barbecued sausages that are served the same way as souvlakia – in pita with shredded cabbage and salad. They are addictive, and easy to make.

SOUVLA

This isn't a formal recipe, more of a guide. There are so many variables, it is easier to explain what it is that you want to achieve than give you exact instructions. Cypriots are fanatical about their souvla, and although it might not be achievable for everyone – you really do need a foukou – it would be criminal not to include it. If you don't have one, check out page 298 for stockists, or try it on a regular barbecue; just make sure there is enough distance between the meat and the coals, and that you turn the meat regularly.

Not everyone marinates their meat before cooking, and it's fine to cook as is, but I do like to if I have time.

SERVES 8

4kg pork or lamb (even chicken can
     be used) – on the bone ideally,
     shoulder or neck is best; get
     your butcher to cut it into large
     chunks for you
olive oil
dried oregano
6 garlic cloves
½ teaspoon sweet smoked paprika
     (optional)
sea salt and freshly ground
     black pepper
3 lemons

Place the meat in a large bowl or non-reactive dish, drizzle over a few glugs of olive oil and add 1 tablespoon of dried oregano. Crush the garlic cloves and add to the bowl with the paprika, if using. Toss together and leave in the fridge for a few hours, or overnight if possible.

Get your barbecue ready and lit; the charcoal needs to be white before you start cooking. Skewer the meat onto large skewers, but don't push the pieces too close together. Reserve the marinade. Place the skewers on the highest setting or grill level, so they are around 25–30cm away from the coals, and turn on the motor. This will mean the meat cooks slowly and the fat will render out while cooking, keeping it moist. Occasionally baste with the oregano marinade and season generously with salt and pepper while cooking. As the meat cooks, bring the skewers slowly closer to the coals, about halfway through.

When the meat is almost ready, squeeze over the juice of 1 of the lemons. The meat is done when it is crispy and gnarly on the outside and tender inside – it can take anything from 1½ to 3 hours depending on the size and cut of your meat and the heat of the coals. Squeeze over more lemon juice for the last 10 minutes, and sprinkle over more oregano. Serve with knives and forks – this isn't a pita bread affair – lots of salads and the remaining lemon cut into wedges.

SOUVLAKIA

I've given you two recipes and split them in terms of servings. The pork one is served in a more traditional Greek way, with round fluffy pita breads, chips and mustard sauce, found throughout Greece. And the chicken recipe is served the Cypriot way: in oval pita breads, with shredded cabbage and griddled olives. However, feel free to interchange the recipes – they'll both work well in either situation.

HERBY PORK SOUVLAKI WITH MUSTARD SAUCE

SERVES 4

2 pork tenderloins, around 400g each
a few sprigs of rosemary
½ a bunch of thyme
2 garlic cloves
sea salt and freshly ground black
   pepper
100ml olive oil
1 tablespoon red wine vinegar
125g Greek yoghurt
3 tablespoons mayonnaise
1 tablespoon honey
1–2 tablespoons English mustard
3 tomatoes
1 red onion
1 lemon
a few sprigs of flat-leaf parsley
4 × round fluffy pita breads (see page
   256 or use shop-bought)
a pinch of sweet smoked paprika
tzatziki (see page 55)
chips (see page 157 if you want to
   make your own)

Cut the pork into even 2–3cm chunks and place in a mixing bowl. Pick and finely chop the rosemary and thyme leaves and add to the pork. Peel and finely grate in the garlic. Season well, then stir in the olive oil and red wine vinegar and cover. Refrigerate and leave to marinate for at least half an hour, longer if possible. If using wooden skewers be sure to soak them in water first to stop them burning.

If you are making chips (see page 157), get them on the go now.

Get the sides ready. To make the mustard sauce, mix together the yoghurt, mayonnaise, honey and mustard to taste. Season to taste, cover and set aside till needed.

Chop the tomatoes and peel and finely slice the onion. Mix them together in a bowl and squeeze over the juice of the lemon. Finely chop the parsley and scatter over the top. Set aside until needed.

When you are ready to cook, preheat a griddle pan to a high heat (or get your barbecue going). Thread 4 large skewers (or 8 small ones) with the marinated pork, being careful not to push the pieces too close together, so that they cook thoroughly all the way through. Cook the meat on the hot griddle pan for around 10–12 minutes, turning evenly, until they are charred and cooked through. Warm the pita breads on the side of the griddle or barbecue for a few minutes at the end. Serve everything together and let everyone build their own kebabs – but be sure to finish with a sprinkle of paprika.

CHICKEN SOUVLAKI, CHILLI SAUCE AND BBQ OLIVES

SERVES 4

800g skinless and boneless
    chicken thighs
300g Greek yoghurt
2 garlic cloves
2 lemons
sea salt and freshly ground
    black pepper
½ teaspoon dried chilli flakes
1 teaspoon dried oregano
olive oil
40 black olives, the wrinkly kind,
    not the ones in brine (although
    you can use these if you can't
    find the dry ones)
1 onion
¼ of a white cabbage
a few sprigs of flat-leaf parsley
3 tomatoes
½ a cucumber
4 pita breads (see page 256
    or use shop-bought)
tzatziki (see page 55)
pickled green chillies
a good chilli sauce (see page 157
    if you want to make your own)

Cut the chicken into even 2–3cm chunks and place in a mixing bowl. Add the yoghurt. Peel and finely grate in the garlic and the zest of one of the lemons. Season well, add the dried chilli and oregano and stir all together with 2 tablespoons of olive oil. Cover, refrigerate and leave to marinate for at least half an hour, longer if possible.

If using wooden skewers be sure to soak them in water first to stop them burning.

Get the sides ready. Push the olives onto skewers. Peel the onion and shred with the cabbage, as finely as you can. Place in a bowl and squeeze over the juice of one of the lemons, then season well. Chop the parsley and toss through the cabbage, then set aside. Slice or chop the tomatoes and cucumber, and toss together.

When you are ready to cook, preheat a griddle pan to a high heat (or get your barbecue going). Thread 4 large skewers (or 8 small ones) with the marinated chicken, being careful not to push the pieces too close together, so that they cook thoroughly all the way through. Cook the meat on the hot griddle pan for around 12 minutes, turning evenly, until they are charred and cooked through.

Griddle the olives at the same time, for around 6 minutes, until toasted and a little crispy. Warm the pita breads on the side of the griddle or barbecue for a few minutes at the end.

Serve the chicken skewers with the warm pita, shredded cabbage, chopped salad, tzatziki, toasted olives and chilli sauce and let everyone build their own kebabs. Be sure to finish with more lemon.

HOMEMADE OVEN CHIPS

This only makes a small quantity, enough for a few chips in the kebabs. If you want more, to eat alongside your meal, then double or triple the quantity.

600g potatoes – Maris Piper
   or King Edwards work best
olive oil
sea salt

Preheat your oven to 230°C/gas mark 8. Bring a large pan of salted water to the boil. Cut the potatoes into chips, around 1cm in thickness. Cook for 2 minutes in the boiling water, then drain in a colander and steam dry over the hot pan.

Place the chips in a large roasting tray, drizzle with olive oil and sprinkle with sea salt. Use your hands to toss everything together, making sure that every piece of potato is coated in seasoned oil. Place in the oven for around 35–40 minutes, turning the chips halfway through, until cooked through, golden and crisp all over.

HOMEMADE CHILLI SAUCE

There are so many chilli sauces available nowadays it's a bit of a minefield. This isn't the most glamorous, the fanciest or the hottest one in the world. But it is incredibly easy, tasty and perfect in a kebab. Keeping things authentic here.

MAKES ABOUT 500G

1–2 red chillies (depending on
   how hot you want your sauce)
½ a red onion
1 garlic clove
1 teaspoon dried chilli flakes
1 × 400g tin of plum tomatoes
1 tablespoon red wine vinegar
2 tablespoons olive oil
1 tablespoon tomato purée
sea salt and freshly ground
   black pepper
½ a bunch of coriander

Halve the chillies and remove the seeds. Peel and roughly chop the onion and garlic. Place them all in a food processor with the chilli flakes and blitz till smooth. Add the plum tomatoes and vinegar and blitz again. Place a medium-sized frying pan on a low heat and drizzle in the olive oil. Fry the tomato purée for a couple of minutes, then add the blitzed tomato-chilli mixture. Cook on a low heat for 10 minutes, until slightly thickened and glossy. Season to taste. Finely chop the coriander, stir through and leave to cool. Transfer to a clean jar and store in the fridge until needed.

SHEFTALIA

These little sausages are basically meatballs wrapped in caul fat. Caul fat is a lacy membrane that protects the internal organs of some animals, and is a traditional sausage casing. It keeps all the moisture and flavours in, and goes deliciously crisp on the barbecue. You'll need to find a good butcher who can order you some.

Serve the sheftalia as you would souvlakia (page 154), in an opened pita with tzatziki (see page 55), lemons, pickles, shredded cabbage (see souvlaki recipe on page 156) and lots of salad. And any sheftalia you don't cook will live happily in the freezer for a few months.

MAKES AROUND 30

500g caul fat
2 lemons, plus extra to serve
2 onions
1 garlic clove
2 ripe tomatoes
1 bunch of parsley
2 teaspoons sea salt
1 teaspoon ground black pepper
1 teaspoon ground cinnamon
½ teaspoon paprika (optional)
1kg pork mince
Small glass of red wine

Wash the caul fat in cold running water, then place it in a large bowl, cover with fresh cold water and squeeze in the juice of the lemons. Leave to one side for 15 minutes.

While the caul is soaking, make the filling. Peel and finely chop the onions and garlic. Place in a large mixing bowl and coarsely grate in the tomatoes, discarding the skins. Finely chop the parsley, stalks and all, and add along with the seasoning and spices. Add the pork mince, a splash of red wine, and mix everything really well with your hands, scrunching it all together.

Drain the caul fat and stretch it out on a clean worktop. Use a tablespoon to spoon large mounds of the mixture onto a corner of the caul fat, then fold in the outside edges and roll it into a small sausage shape – the same way you'd roll koupepia (see page 81). Use a knife to cut out the sheftalia and place on a large tray. Keep going until all the mixture has been used.

The best way to cook sheftalia is slowly over a barbecue, alternatively you can cook them in the oven. Be warned, they release a lot of fat. Either skewer them on two skewers to keep them rigid or place them in a grill basket, and turn them halfway through cooking. They take around 10–12 minutes on each side. You want to make sure they are cooked through, and that the caul fat has melted away to leave a crispy exterior. Serve with lemon wedges, pita, pickles and salad.

MY MAMA'S AVGOLEMONI SOUP

To those who have never tried it, this may sound odd, but trust me when I say it is the most delicious, comforting, warming meal you will have. It also feels greatly healing and medicinal, and it's what's made when someone is poorly or run down.

So what is different about my mum's recipe that makes it the greatest of them all? (Yes, I am hugely biased.) She makes the creamiest soup by using a free-standing mixer to whisk the hot stock into the eggs. When she was a little girl, her mum, my yiayia, would get her to whisk it all together. One day, with tired arms, she had the genius idea of using her much-prized Kenwood mixer (which she still has to this day). If you don't have one, don't worry, just whisk everything together for longer than you think – until it is a little foamy. The ratio of ingredients is also important, yielding a thicker, creamier soup. It's best if you can poach a chicken and use the homemade chicken stock, but if you don't have time, a really good quality bought chicken stock is OK, too.

SERVES 6

If you go for the poached
  chicken option:

1 × 1.6kg chicken

1 bay leaf

a few peppercorns

2 onions

2 sticks of celery

2 carrots

Alternatively you will need 2.5 litres
  of good chicken stock

225g long-grain rice

4 large eggs

2 lemons

½ teaspoon ground cinnamon

sea salt and freshly ground
  black pepper

If you're poaching a chicken, place the bird in a large saucepan and pop in the bay leaf and peppercorns. Peel and roughly chop the onions, roughly chop the celery and carrots and add everything to the pot. Place on a high heat, bring to the boil, then reduce the heat to low, cover with a lid and simmer for around 1 hour until the chicken is tender and falling apart. Remove the bird and leave to one side to cool, then refrigerate and keep for another time. Strain the veg and flavourings out of the stock and measure the liquid; you need around 2.5 litres.

If you are not poaching your own bird, start here. Place the chicken stock in the saucepan and bring to the boil over a high heat. Stir in the rice, then reduce the heat and cook for 20 minutes, until the rice is soft. Turn off the heat. Meanwhile, crack the eggs into the bowl of a free-standing mixer and squeeze in the juice of 1½ lemons. Add the cinnamon and a generous pinch of salt and pepper and whisk everything together well. (If you don't have a free-standing mixer, use a large mixing bowl and either an electric hand whisk or a regular whisk.) With the mix running on slow, ladle in some hot chicken stock (but no rice), whisking it into the eggs thoroughly until creamy. Repeat 3 more times, with the motor running the whole time, until you have a glossy mixture. Then pour the egg and stock mixture back into the pan with the rice. Turn the heat on to low, and simmer for 4–5 minutes, until you have a thick, creamy soup. Stir constantly so that it doesn't catch or scramble. Taste and add the remaining lemon, if you like, and tweak the seasoning. Serve straight away, with extra ground cinnamon on the side.

CHICKEN, CINNAMON AND SWEET TOMATO ORZO: *KOTOPOULO KRITHARAKI*

There are so many versions of kritharaki (orzo) in Greek and Cypriot cooking – it is a huge staple for us, and almost always cooked with tomato. This chicken dish is the sort of family one-pot recipe all households should have up their sleeve. I'd put a bet on it being a winner with all ages.

SERVES 4–6

1 litre chicken stock
2 onions
2 garlic cloves
olive oil
1 stick of cinnamon
1 tablespoon tomato purée
5 ripe tomatoes
400g orzo
6 chicken thighs, on the bone
    and skin on
½ teaspoon ground allspice
sea salt and freshly ground
    black pepper
250g cherry tomatoes on the vine
6 sprigs of fresh oregano
75g halloumi or salted anari/ricotta

Preheat your oven to 200°C/gas mark 6. Heat the chicken stock. Peel and finely chop the onions and garlic. Pour 3 tablespoons of olive oil into a wide casserole pan and add the chopped veg. Place on a medium low heat and sauté for 10 minutes, until starting to soften. Add the cinnamon stick and tomato purée to the pan and stir for a minute. Coarsely grate in the large tomatoes, give everything a stir, then stir in the orzo and hot stock.

Toss the chicken thighs with the allspice and a generous pinch of salt and pepper. Place the chicken on top of the orzo, skin side up, and dot around the vines of tomatoes and sprigs of oregano. Drizzle everything with olive oil and place in the oven for around 30 minutes.

Towards the end of this cooking time, boil a kettle. When 30 minutes is up, remove the casserole pan from the oven. Carefully pour 150ml of boiling water all around the orzo (not on the chicken skin) and return to the oven. Cook for a further 25 minutes, or until the chicken skin is crisp and golden, and the meat is tender.

Remove from the oven, leave it to rest for 5 minutes, then serve, grating over the cheese.

Served with lemon roast potatoes
and artichokes (page 211)

CORIANDER AND LEMON ROAST CHICKEN

For meat eaters, being presented with a whole roast chicken must surely be one of life's great pleasures. The smell, the crispy, salty skin, the juices in the tray... This simple butter transforms chicken into something a little more exotic. It takes minutes to make but is a real crowd pleaser and will fit in perfectly with your normal Sunday roast routine.

SERVES 4

2 garlic cloves
1 tablespoon coriander seeds
½ teaspoon cumin seeds
a bunch of coriander
50g unsalted butter
2 tablespoons olive oil
sea salt and freshly ground
    black pepper
2 lemons
1 × 1.6kg chicken

Peel the garlic cloves. Gently crush the coriander and cumin seeds in a pestle and mortar, then place in a mini chopper or powerful blender with the fresh coriander and garlic and pulse till finely chopped. Add the butter, olive oil, a good pinch of salt and pepper and finely grate in the zest of both the lemons. Blitz together until you have a vibrant green paste.

Preheat your oven to 190°C/gas mark 5. Gently prise the skin away from the chicken neck and breast and rub the coriander butter underneath and all over the skin. Rub it all over the chicken, including the thighs and wings, until it is completely coated. Place in a small roasting tray. Halve one of the lemons and pop it into the cavity. Place the tray in the oven and roast for about an hour and 10 minutes, basting occasionally with the juices in the tray and squeezing over the juice of the remaining lemon. It is ready when it is golden and crisp and the juices around the thighs run clear when pierced. Leave to rest for 10 minutes, then serve in the tray with the buttery juices.

—

SPICY SAUSAGE AND PEPPER STEW: *SPETSOFAI*

Unlike a lot of Greek meat dishes, this is one that is easily achievable after a busy day. Traditionally it would be made with loukanika, slightly spicy Greek sausages. However, they aren't readily available everywhere, so feel free to make this with any good-quality pork sausage you can find – Italian sausages tend to have a pepperiness to them that works well. Also, totally untraditional, but any leftovers make a fantastic breakfast. Topped with a poached egg and a side of toast, it is a brunch fit for royalty.

SERVES 4

8 loukanika or good pork sausages
   (ones that are a little spicy
   work well)
4 large red peppers
2 large green peppers
2 pale green chilli peppers (the
   long yellowish-green kind you
   find in most international grocers;
   alternatively use an extra regular
   green pepper)
1–2 red chillies
2 red onions
3 ripe tomatoes
olive oil
1 tablespoon tomato purée
75ml red wine
sea salt and freshly ground
   black pepper
a splash of red wine vinegar
fresh bread and feta (optional),
   to serve

Cut the sausages into large pieces, around 3–4cm long. Halve and deseed all the peppers, then cut into large chunks or slices (I like a mixture of shapes). Halve, deseed and finely slice the chillies. Peel, halve and finely slice the onions. Finely chop the tomatoes.

Place a large, wide saucepan on a medium heat and drizzle in a little olive oil. Fry the sausages for about 5 minutes, until they start to brown. Using a slotted spoon, remove them from the pan and leave them to one side. Add all the chopped peppers, chillies and onions to the pan and reduce the heat slightly. Sauté them for 15 minutes in the sausage fat, until softened and sticky. Stir in the tomato purée, cook for a couple of minutes, then add the red wine. Turn the heat up a little and bring the wine to the boil, reducing it almost all away. Return the browned sausages to the pan with the chopped tomatoes and season. Turn up the heat, bring to a simmer, then reduce the heat to low, cover with a lid and cook for around 25 minutes, until the peppers have cooked down and the sausages are cooked through. Stir through a splash of red wine vinegar and serve straight away, with a loaf of fresh bread and a block of feta for crumbling over – if you like.

PORK IN RED WINE, CORIANDER AND MUSHROOMS: *AFELIA*

Afelia feels like quite an old-fashioned dish; it's not something that I've seen around for a while and I really don't know why. Granted, it feels more autumnal and wintery than a lot of other Greek foods, but for those of us that don't live under the Mediterranean sun it is a dream. Familiar almost. A side of hot buttery mashed potato would be totally unauthentic but so well suited.

SERVES 4–6

1.25kg boneless and skinless
  pork shoulder
2 tablespoons coriander seeds
olive oil
200ml red wine
150ml commandaria – Cypriot
  sweet red wine (or just use more
  normal red wine)
1 bunch of spring onions
2 garlic cloves
500g mushrooms – chestnut
  or a mixture
2 tablespoons plain flour
300ml chicken or beef stock
sea salt and freshly ground
  black pepper
a splash of double cream (optional)

You'll need to start this the night, or at least the morning, before you intend to cook it. Cut the pork into chunks around 4cm and place in a large mixing bowl. Crush the coriander seeds in a pestle and mortar, not too finely, and add to the bowl along with 2 tablespoons of olive oil and both the red wines (if using). Stir everything together and cover the bowl, then pop into the fridge to marinate.

When you are ready to cook the afelia, place a large casserole or saucepan on a medium heat. Drizzle in a little olive oil and brown the meat on all sides (you may need to do this in batches), reserving the marinade. Meanwhile trim and slice the spring onions, and peel and finely slice the garlic. Wipe the mushrooms clean and roughly chop them. When the pork is all browned, spoon it all back into the pan and stir in the chopped veg. Reduce the heat a little and fry for 5 minutes, then stir in the flour, so it coats everything. After a minute add the wine marinade and bring to the boil.

Cook over a medium heat until the wine has reduced by half, then top up with just enough stock to cover the meat and veg. Bring back to the boil, cover the pan, reduce the heat, then simmer over a very low heat for around 2 hours, until the meat is tender and falling apart. Check the stew occasionally, giving it a stir and adding a splash of boiling water if it gets a little dry.

When it is ready, the pork should melt in the mouth and the sauce should be thick. If it needs thickening a little, remove the lid and cook uncovered for 10 minutes. Season generously and add a splash of double cream before serving, if you wish.

SLOW-ROASTED PORK SHOULDER WITH QUINCE: *HIRINO ME KIDONI*

The combination of salty, fatty pork, crisp crackling and sweet stewed quince works perfectly, making this is one of my favourite Sunday dinners. Traditionally this would be more of a stew, made with chunks of pork; however, a larger piece of meat makes a great feast centrepiece. I also use white wine, so that the ingredients are able to sing a little more and are not too masked by the intensity of a red wine, but feel free to try either – the quantities and method are the same.

SERVES 6

sea salt and freshly ground black
    pepper
2.2kg rolled, boned pork shoulder –
    skin scored by your butcher
½ bunch of thyme
olive oil
2 onions
1 orange
800g quince
200ml chicken stock
1 stick of cinnamon
6 cloves
175ml dry white wine, or apple juice

Turn your oven to full whack, and leave it to get nice and hot. Season the pork generously, pick over the thyme leaves and poke in some of the sprigs. Drizzle over a little olive oil and rub all seasoning into the meat and between the scores in the skin. Place the pork on a roasting tray that's big enough to hold all the ingredients later on, and place it in the oven for 30 minutes so that the skin has a chance to crackle.

While the pork is in the oven, prepare the rest of the ingredients. Peel and finely slice the onions. Use a potato peeler to peel 4 thick slices of orange zest. Peel, core and slice the quince into 2cm wedges (if you do this in advance, be sure to place them in a large bowl of cold water and squeeze over some lemon juice to stop them discolouring). Heat the chicken stock.

When the pork has had half an hour, remove the tray from the oven and reduce the oven temperature to 140°C/gas mark 1. Remove the pork from the tray and pop in the sliced quince, onion, orange zest, cinnamon stick and cloves. Pour over the wine and hot stock and place the pork on top. Cover the pork and tray with foil and return to the oven for 4 hours, or until the meat is tender. Check on it occasionally and top up with water if the base is getting a little dry. Once the pork is ready and tender, remove the foil, turn the heat back up to 220°C/gas mark 7 and pop the tray back in for 30 minutes, to get the crackling crispy again. Be sure to add a little more hot water to stop the quince drying out – there should be a little liquid in the bottom. Remove from the oven, leave the meat to rest for 15 minutes, then serve.

PASTITSIO: *MAKARONIA TOU FOURNOU*

Growing up we never called this pastitsio, and to be honest I had no idea it had a different name in Greece – we've always called it makaronia tou fourno, which literally translates as 'pasta (macaroni) in the oven'. It is perfect for a large gathering – not necessarily the most elegant meal but a crowd pleaser that needs to be made ahead of time and left to 'sit' and firm up (i.e. not served hot).

I've since looked into why we don't serve it hot and there are several thoughts, one being that, like lasagne, it is so that the layers firm up. The other being that traditionally people couldn't afford ovens in their homes so they would send their trays to the local 'fourno' (bakery), where they would bake them en masse. By the time they were ready and returned to their homes they had cooled down. (I can definitely imagine this happening as I've sent things to the local fourno before, usually around Easter when we are making breads by the trayload.)

Two unusual tips here. First, use a little baking powder in the béchamel. This is my Yiayia Martha's tip, and she swears it makes the béchamel a little lighter. The other is to add a little of the white sauce to the ragù before you layer it up. It helps it to set the whole dish, and make it creamy overall.

SERVES 8, GENEROUSLY

150g halloumi or salted ricotta
2 onions
2 garlic cloves
olive oil
1 tablespoon tomato purée
750g mince (Greeks from Greece
    tend to use beef, whilst Cypriots
    tend to use pork. I prefer pork,
    or even a blend of the two)
1 teaspoon ground cinnamon
1 stick of cinnamon
2 bay leaves
2 ripe tomatoes
300ml beef stock
500g pasta – mezzani 'A' or bucatini
½ a bunch of flat-leaf parsley
3 large eggs
1.6 litres milk
160g unsalted butter
160g plain flour
1 heaped teaspoon baking powder
sea salt and freshly ground
    black pepper

Finely grate the cheese and leave to one side.

Peel and finely chop the onions and garlic. Place a large saucepan on a medium-low heat and drizzle in a tablespoon of olive oil. Add the chopped veg and sauté until softened but not coloured, for about 10 minutes. Add the tomato purée, stir for a minute, then add the mince and ground cinnamon. Turn up the heat a little and fry for a few minutes, breaking up the mince with a wooden spoon, then add the cinnamon stick and bay leaves. Coarsely grate in the tomatoes and discard the skins. Pour in the beef stock, bring to the boil, then reduce to low and simmer uncovered for 30 minutes, until the liquid has almost all reduced. The meat should be slightly wet, but not 'runny'.

Preheat your oven to 180°C/gas mark 4.

Meanwhile place a large pan of salted water on to boil and cook the pasta for 2 minutes less than packet instructions. When it is ready, drain and drizzle in a little olive oil. Finely chop the parsley and add to the pasta. Whisk 1 of the eggs and toss through with a handful of the grated cheese. Keep to one side.

Warm the milk. Make the béchamel by melting the butter in a large saucepan. Stir in the flour and baking powder until you have a paste, then pour in just enough milk to loosen, whisking it in. Keep going, adding the milk gradually and whisking it in each time till you have a smooth white sauce. Add half the remaining grated cheese and season to taste. Crack in the remaining 2 eggs and whisk in.

To layer up the pastitsio, you'll need a deep 25cm × 35cm roasting tray or earthenware dish. Whisk one ladleful of the white sauce into the ragù. Spread half the pasta in the bottom of the tray and top with half the ragù (discarding the cinnamon stick and bay leaves). Repeat with the remaining pasta and ragù. Finish by pouring over the white sauce, and scattering over the remaining grated cheese.

Place the tray in the oven and bake for about 45 minutes, until golden on top and bubbling. Remove from the oven and leave the pastitsio to cool for at least 30 minutes before slicing and serving.

CLASSIC MOUSSAKA

Moussaka is one of those dishes about which everyone has a story, a variation, and an opinion – meat being the main culprit. People think that the meat in most of our dishes is lamb, but in my family (and for a lot of other Greeks and Cypriots) the meat in moussaka is pork. Veal was used, too, but less so now. As a result, when I make moussaka I use a mixture of beef and pork, but I've left the option open here. Some people love lamb – it's up to you. Also, I've always made my moussaka with baked vegetables. My yiayias used to make it the traditional way, frying the slices of aubergine, potato and courgette; however, as times changed, fried foods became rarer. (Aubergines really are little sponges and will guzzle all the oil you give them.) And now we mostly bake or grill them. Still delicious, I promise you.

Served here with village salad (page

SERVES 6–8

700g potatoes

3 aubergines

olive oil

sea salt and freshly ground
    black pepper

2 courgettes

3 onions

4 garlic cloves

2 teaspoon ground cinnamon

1½ teaspoons dried oregano

500g mince (see intro)

2 tablespoons tomato purée

200ml red wine

400ml passata

1 bay leaf

1 stick of cinnamon

1.25 litre milk

100g unsalted butter

125g plain flour

1 teaspoon baking powder

80g kefalotyri or pecorino

nutmeg, for grating

3 eggs

Preheat your oven to 180°C/gas mark 4. Peel the potatoes. Slice some of the aubergine skin off in strips (see page 13). Slice them both into ½cm rounds. Lay them all out on a couple of baking or roasting trays and brush with olive oil. Season and roast in the oven for 35–40 minutes, until golden. Remove and set aside. Trim and finely slice the courgettes and keep to one side.

Meanwhile, peel and finely chop the onions and garlic. Pour a couple of tablespoons of olive oil into a large saucepan over a medium-low heat. Sauté the onions and garlic for 10 minutes, until starting to soften. Add the ground cinnamon, oregano and all the mince. Break everything up with a wooden spoon and turn the heat up a little. Fry until any liquid evaporates and it starts to turn lightly brown. Stir in the purée, then add the wine and bring to the boil. Leave to rapidly simmer for 5 minutes, until the wine has reduced by more than half, then stir in the passata, bay leaf and cinnamon stick. Season generously, bring to the boil, then reduce to a simmer and cook on a low heat for 30 minutes, until thickened and reduced.

Heat the milk in a small pan. Melt the butter in a large saucepan over a medium heat and stir in the flour and baking powder. Once they have made a paste, slowly start to whisk in the warmed milk, until you have a smooth white sauce. Leave it to thicken over a low heat until it coats the back of a spoon. Grate in half the cheese and a generous amount of nutmeg. Season to taste.

When the meat and white sauce are ready, layer up the moussaka. You'll need a large roasting tray, about 25cm × 30cm in size. Layer a third of the baked veg and courgettes in the base of the tray and spoon over half of the mince. Repeat with half the remaining veg, the rest of the mince and then the last of the vegetables. Whisk the eggs into the white sauce and pour over the moussaka. Grate over the remaining cheese and place the dish in the oven. Bake for 45 minutes, or until the top is golden and bubbling and everything is cooked through. Remove from the oven and leave to cool for at least 15 minutes before serving, if not longer.

BEEF, RED WINE AND BABY ONION STEW: *STIFADO*

This is the kind of wintery stew that is incredibly forgiving. Cook it lower, slower, add potatoes (I do), use leftovers in a pie... It never felt like a particularly exciting dish growing up, but now it is the food I crave on a cold, lazy Sunday.

SERVES 4

500g baby onions
500g Cyprus potatoes, or other
   waxy potatoes
olive oil
800g braising beef, cut in
   4 large pieces
½ teaspoon ground allspice
2 tablespoons tomato purée
175ml red wine
400ml beef stock
2 tablespoons red wine vinegar
a few sprigs of thyme
2 bay leaves
1 stick of cinnamon
4 cloves
3 ripe tomatoes
sea salt and freshly ground
   black pepper

Preheat your oven to 160°C/gas mark 3.

Peel the onions, keeping them whole if possible (you can do this by pouring boiling water over them to help peel away the skin). Scrub the potatoes and cut into large chunks, around 4cm, and set aside. Place a large casserole dish on a medium heat and drizzle in a good few table-spoons of olive oil. Brown the meat on all sides, then remove the beef to a plate and set aside. Add the peeled onions to the casserole and fry for about 5 minutes, until they begin to soften. Stir in the ground allspice and tomato purée and fry for a minute, then add the red wine and bring to the boil. Reduce the heat a little and leave it bubbling to reduce the wine. After 5–10 minutes, the wine should have halved, so pour in the stock and vinegar, and add the thyme sprigs, bay leaves, cinnamon and cloves.

Chop the tomatoes and add to the casserole with the beef, potatoes and a generous pinch of salt and pepper. Bring everything to the boil, then cover with a lid and transfer the casserole to the oven. Cook for 3 hours, or until the meat is tender and falling apart (the exact time will depend on what meat you have chosen and how large you have cut it). When the meat is tender, remove the lid and cook for a further 20 minutes uncovered. Keep an eye on the liquid and make sure it doesn't dry out, adding a splash of water if needed.

When it is ready, taste and tweak the seasoning, adding a little more vinegar if it needs it.

CRISPY LAMB CHOPS AND A CYPRIOT SALSA VERDE

One of my favourite memories of my Yiayia Maroulla's kitchen is when she would cook lamb chops. The smell was divine and my mum was always caught red-handed by the oven, eating the crispy fat before we'd had a chance to sit down. As I've mentioned before, Cypriot meat recipes can be quite laborious but these are another weeknight staple. I serve them with a Cypriot-inspired salsa verde – it's so easy and complements the meat beautifully.

SERVES 2

½ tablespoon sesame seeds
½ teaspoon cumin seeds
2 garlic cloves
1 lemon
extra virgin olive oil
4–6 lamb cutlets, depending on size
sea salt and freshly ground
    black pepper
1 green chilli
½ a bunch of flat-leaf parsley
½ a bunch of mint
½ a bunch of coriander
1 tablespoon capers
4 anchovy fillets
2 tablespoons red wine vinegar
2 flatbreads

Toast the sesame and cumin seeds in a small dry pan and leave to one side. Peel the garlic cloves. Finely grate one of them into a shallow mixing bowl (big enough to hold all the lamb cutlets) and finely grate in the zest of the lemon. Squeeze in the lemon juice, drizzle in a little extra virgin olive oil and season well. Add the lamb, toss to coat, cover and leave in the fridge to marinate until needed (the longer you can leave it the better).

Halve and deseed the chilli and finely chop on a large chopping board with the remaining garlic clove. Pick the herb leaves and add to the board along with the capers and anchovies. Chop everything together finely. Spoon it all into a mixing bowl and stir in the red wine vinegar and enough extra virgin olive oil to loosen.

Place a griddle pan on a high heat. Toast the flatbreads till nicely charred, then tear them and lay over a large platter. Spoon over the salsa verde. Griddle the lamb cutlets for around 4–5 minutes on each side, until gnarled and crisp on the outside but still a little pink in the middle (griddle for a couple of minutes longer if you like them well done). Pile the cutlets on top of the salsa verde and flatbreads and serve sprinkled with the toasted seeds. Serve straight away.

STOLEN LAMB WITH OREGANO POTATOES: *KLEFTIKO*

The thing with very old, traditional recipes is that everyone has their inherited version. I've sat through arguments between Greek people where one person swears blind kleftiko has to have cinnamon in, whilst another scoffs at the idea. Who is to say who is right? Some chop the meat, others leave it whole, sometimes leg, sometimes shoulder... I've even seen versions with cheese. This is our version, and I hope you like it.

SERVES 6

1 leg or shoulder of lamb, around
   2kg – you can ask your butcher
   to cut it into 4 large pieces,
   or leave it whole
olive oil
sea salt and freshly ground
   black pepper
½ tablespoon dried oregano
3 bay leaves
1 bulb of garlic
1kg Cyprus potatoes (or Maris Pipers)
2 onions
4 ripe tomatoes
1 stick of cinnamon
a few sprigs of fresh oregano
   (optional)
2 lemons
250ml white wine

You will need a roll of baking paper
*   for this recipe*

Start the day before by marinating the lamb. Place it in a large dish and drizzle over some olive oil. Season generously, sprinkle over the oregano, and crush in the bay leaves. Peel 2 garlic cloves and cut each into 4 pieces. Pierce the lamb 8 times with a sharp knife and poke in the garlic. Rub in all the flavours and cover the dish. Place in the fridge overnight.

Take the lamb out of the fridge 20 minutes before you want to cook your kleftiko. Preheat the oven to 160°C/gas mark 3. Line a large roasting tray big enough to hold all the ingredients with baking paper, and make sure there is enough of an overhang to crimp the edges (you might need to fold 2 pieces together lengthways to make sure it is wide enough).

Wash the potatoes, removing any dirt, and cut them into long chunks or thick wedges. Peel the onions and cut into thin wedges. Crush the remaining unpeeled garlic cloves with the flat of your knife. Roughly chop the tomatoes. Place all the veg in the tray on the paper and poke in the cinnamon stick and fresh oregano sprigs, if using. Place the marinated lamb on top and spoon over the juices in the bowl. Squeeze over the juice of the lemons and pour the wine into the bottom of the dish. Tear off another sheet of paper and wet it under running water. Squeeze out the excess and lay it over the lamb, crimping the edges of the paper together with the pieces underneath (it needs to be completely sealed). Place the tray in the oven and leave it, untouched, for 3 hours. If you are using a whole piece of lamb, unchopped, it will need to cook for at least 4½ hours.

Once the lamb is cooked and very tender, remove the top sheet of paper. Turn the oven up to 200°C/gas mark 6, and return the tray for a final 15 minutes, to give it a little colour. Leave the meat to rest for 10 minutes, before serving with all the vegetables and juices from the tray.

THEIA FROSA'S *TAVA*

Every Cypriot family has their own version of tava, and I learnt this one from my adorable Aunt Frosa. Slow-cooked lamb that melts in the mouth... It's an easy, throw-it-all-together, one-pot wonder and I've never met a meat eater who doesn't love it. If you are lucky enough to have a wood or clay oven, then by all means cook it in there, it will be heaven-sent. For the rest of us, a domestic oven still works pretty darn great.

SERVES 4–6

4 onions
800g Cyprus potatoes
900g lamb neck fillet
80ml good olive oil
1 tablespoon ground cumin
3 bay leaves
2 tablespoons tomato purée
sea salt and freshly ground black
   pepper
6 ripe tomatoes
75g long-grain rice
350ml hot chicken stock
½ a bunch of flat-leaf parsley

Preheat your oven to 160°C/gas mark 3. Peel the onions and cut into thin wedges. Peel the potatoes and cut into large chunks, around 4cm. Cut the lamb to a similar size. Place in a large earthenware dish or casserole with half the olive oil, the cumin, bay leaves and tomato purée. Season generously and massage everything together with your hands. Roughly chop the tomatoes and stir into the lamb, along with the rice and hot stock. Cover the dish with foil or the lid and place in the oven for 2½ hours, checking a couple of times and adding a little extra stock, or hot water, if need be.

When the dish is ready, the lamb should be melt-in-the-mouth soft and the potatoes cooked through. If it's not quite there, cover the dish and return it to the oven for a further 20 minutes. When it is perfectly cooked, remove the lid or foil and turn the oven up to 200°C/gas mark 6. Drizzle the surface of the tava with the remaining olive oil, and return it to the oven for a further 20 minutes, until caramelised and browned. Finely chop the parsley, stir through and serve.

SLOW-COOKED LAMB SHOULDER WITH FRESH DATES

My Aunts Frosa and Vasso have huge date trees in their gardens, and Frosa's is so big she had to ask the entire village to come and take the fresh dates last year – there was no way our (enormous) family could get through them all. It got me thinking how you could use the fresh variety in cooking, as they are sweet but not as tooth-achingly sweet as the dried variety found in supermarkets.

In the UK, you can find fresh dates in Greek and Middle Eastern shops in late summer. They're worth buying in bulk, as they freeze beautifully, becoming even a little sweeter. If you can't find fresh dates, use 300g of medjool dates with the stones removed, and 300g of peeled, chopped orchard fruits like apples and pears.

I use lamb shoulder in this recipe as it's so readily available. However Greeks and Cypriots love eating goat and if you were to do this recipe with goat shoulder – if you can find it – it would be delicious.

SERVES 6

1 × 2kg lamb shoulder
600g fresh dates
4 red onions
6 garlic cloves
4 bay leaves
1 small stick of cinnamon
olive oil
sea salt and freshly ground
  black pepper
500ml hot beef or chicken stock
2 tablespoons date molasses
a splash of red wine vinegar

Preheat the oven to 160°C/gas mark 3. Take your lamb shoulder out of the fridge 20 minutes before you want to cook it. While it is coming up to room temperature, halve the dates and remove the stones (this is easy to do if you cut them through the stem). Peel the onions and slice into 1cm wedges. Crush the garlic with the skins on, using the side of a chef's knife.

When the lamb is ready, pierce it in 4 places and poke in the bay leaves. Scatter the dates, cinnamon stick, onions and garlic in a large roasting tray and place the lamb on top. Drizzle with a little olive oil, season generously, then pour the hot stock into the tray. Take a large piece of baking paper, run it under cold water, scrunch it up and tuck it over the top of the lamb. Tightly cover the tray with foil and place in the oven for 4 hours.

After 4 hours, remove the foil and paper and drizzle the lamb with the date molasses. Return it to the oven and cook for a further 45 minutes to 1 hour, until the lamb is sticky and incredibly tender, and the stock has reduced. Finish by adding a splash of red wine vinegar to the cooked-down dates and onions, season to taste, then serve. It's perfect alongside a bowl of steaming bulgur wheat or coriander roasted potatoes.

6

SIDES

OLIVE LEMON DRESSING: *LADOLEMONO*

Ladolemono combines the most simple and traditional Greek flavours. It is our most used marinade – almost anything cooked on a BBQ will be marinated then basted in this. If in doubt, douse whatever you are eating in ladolemono and all will be good in the world. It feels a bit mad including a recipe for something that is so made so instinctively, but not to would be sacrilege.

MAKES ABOUT 150ML

3 lemons
100ml extra virgin olive oil
½ teaspoon dried oregano
sea salt and freshly ground
    black pepper

Squeeze the lemons – you want around 50ml of juice – and discard any pips. Whisk in the rest of the ingredients and season to taste. If using as a dressing for salad or vegetables, season a little more than you think. Alternatively, use to baste kebabs, meat or fish on the barbecue.

ARTICHOKES AND KOHLRABI: *ANGINARES KAI KOULOUMBRA*

Not a recipe, rather a nod of recognition. No family dinner was complete without a plate of sliced kouloumbra (kohlrabi), raw globe artichokes and a mound of lemon halves. For years we had no idea what kouloumbra even was in English, but it has always been a fixture. It's peeled, sliced quite crudely, around 1cm thick, then doused in lemon and lots of salt. The raw artichoke petals would be finished the same way, and then eaten by scraping the base of the leaves against our teeth, eating the flesh. The finished table would be happily adorned with dissected artichokes, mounds of squeezed lemons and salt everywhere.

AVOCADO RADISH SALAD IN A TOASTED SESAME DRESSING

Avocados are found in abundance in Cyprus, but they're never made a huge song and dance about. They're often added to salads, or in my dad's case, sprinkled with sugar and eaten straight up. Growing up, I thought this was very strange but turns out he was onto something, with avocado appearing to be the most versatile ingredient of the 21st century. Personally, this is my favourite way to eat it, in a crunchy, crisp salad with a slightly punchy dressing. Delicious.

SERVES 4

2 tablespoons sesame seeds
1 garlic clove
1 lemon
3 tablespoons extra virgin olive oil
1 heaped tablespoon tahini
sea salt and freshly ground
   black pepper
4 spring onions
½ a bunch of mint
250g radishes (whatever type
   you like, breakfast are popular
   in Cyprus and watermelon are
   delicious and beautiful, too)
2 little gem lettuces or
   1 romaine lettuce
2 avocados

Toast the sesame seeds in a dry frying pan over a medium-low heat until golden. Then pour into a bowl and leave to one side. Peel the garlic clove and crush with the side of your knife. Place it in a jam jar or small mixing bowl, and squeeze in the juice of the lemon, discarding the pips. Pour in the extra virgin olive oil, add the tahini and shake or whisk until emulsified, adding water as needed to loosen. Season generously and stir in just over half the sesame seeds.

Trim and finely slice the spring onions. Pick and roughly chop the mint leaves. Trim the radishes and cut them in a variety of ways – I like to finely slice some and roughly chop others. Trim and wash the lettuce leaves. Dry them well, then roughly chop any larger ones and leave the little ones whole. Toss all the chopped veg and herbs together in a bowl. Halve the avocados, and use a teaspoon to scoop little nuggets into the salad. Dress with the tahini dressing, discarding the garlic clove. Finish with any leftover mint and the reserved toasted sesame seeds. Serve straight away.

SHREDDED CABBAGE SLAW: *KRAMBOSALATA*

This is one of my mum's classics, something we would eat regularly growing up. It's so simple and adds much needed freshness to meaty or hearty meals. The key is crisp white cabbage, generously seasoned – don't be shy – and a shedload of lemon juice for tartness and to soften the onions. It's heavenly on a summer's day. (Photo on page 155.)

SERVES 6

1 small white cabbage, around 500g
2 onions
2 lemons
extra virgin olive oil
sea salt and freshly ground
   black pepper

Quarter the cabbage and remove the outer leaves. Cut out most of the core and shred the cabbage as finely as you can. If you have a food processor with a fine slicing attachment, by all means use that. Peel and finely slice the onions and mix them with the cabbage in a bowl. Squeeze over the juice of both the lemons, drizzle with a few tablespoons of extra virgin olive oil and season generously. Toss it all together, making sure everything is well coated in dressing, and set aside for at least 30 minutes before serving.

VILLAGE SALAD: *HORIATIKI SALATA*

An absolute classic. Eating a village salad in Greece or Cyprus – where the tomatoes are sweet, the feta is especially creamy and tangy and the olives are intense – is a meal fit for the gods. (Photo on page 176.)

SERVES 4, AS A SIDE

½ a red onion
1 tablespoon red wine vinegar
500g ripe tomatoes
1 small Greek or Lebanese cucumber
   (or ½ a regular cucumber)
1 green pepper
16 black Kalamata olives
sea salt and freshly ground
   black pepper
3 tablespoons extra virgin olive oil
150g feta
¼ teaspoon dried oregano

Peel and finely slice the red onion. Place in a large bowl with the red wine vinegar and set aside for 5 minutes. Roughly chop and slice the tomatoes. Trim and slice the cucumber and pepper, discarding the pepper seeds. Place the chopped veg in the mixing bowl and tear in the olives, discarding the stones. Season well and toss together with the extra virgin olive oil. Transfer to a platter and top with the feta. Sprinkle over the oregano and serve straight away.

PICKLED ONION PETALS

This is a Turkish Cypriot influenced dish, and something I make religiously to have with souvlaki. It's hugely addictive and I guarantee that you'll have friends flocking for the recipe. (Photo on page 155.)

SERVES 6

2 large red onions
5 tablespoons good-quality
  red wine vinegar
2 tablespoons pomegranate molasses
a pinch of sea salt
½ a bunch of mint
2 tablespoons pomegranate seeds

Make this the day before you plan to serve it, if you can.

Place a griddle pan on a high heat. Trim and peel the onions and cut each one into quarters through the root. Peel each layer away and place the 'petals' on the hot griddle pan, curved side down. (You'll need to do this in a few stages.) Griddle the onion petals for around 5 minutes on the curved side, then turn over for 1 minute on the other side, so they are lightly charred all over. As soon as they're finished, transfer them to a small non-reactive bowl (glass or ceramic) and douse with the vinegar and pomegranate molasses. Keep adding the charred onions to the bowl as they're ready. When all the onions are charred, toss everything together well with a good pinch of salt. Cover the bowl and leave to one side for at least an hour to marinate.

Just before you are ready to serve, pick and roughly chop the mint leaves. Stir the mint and pomegranate seeds through the pickled onions and you're ready to go.

SPICE-ROASTED SQUASH WITH DRIED CHERRIES AND TAHINI

This is a combination of some of my favourite Cypriot flavours. I love squash and pumpkin spiked with cinnamon and paired with sweet dried berries – it's a combination we use in a few dishes. This salad is a play on that, but finished with sumac, which I only came to learn about later in life. It isn't something my yiayias ever used, although it is grown in Cyprus. If you haven't used it before, don't be put off by the red colour – it isn't at all spicy or hot, and adds a wonderful fruity, tangy kick.

SERVES 4-6

1.2kg butternut squash
olive oil
sea salt and freshly ground
   black pepper
1 teaspoon dried oregano
½ teaspoon ground cinnamon
1 heaped tablespoon tahini
1 lemon
80g yoghurt
2–3 tablespoons extra virgin olive oil
6 spring onions
½ a bunch of mint
60g rocket
40g dried cherries
sumac (optional)

Preheat the oven to 200°C/gas mark 6. Cut the squash in half lengthways, then slice into 2–3cm long wedges. Clean out and discard the orange membranes but keep the seeds, giving them a little wash. Place the squash in a roasting tray, so it can all be spread out in one layer, and drizzle with olive oil. Season and sprinkle over the oregano and cinnamon. Toss everything together to coat evenly and pop the tray into the oven for 20 minutes. After 20 minutes, dress the seeds with a little olive oil and salt, and sprinkle over the squash. Roast the squash for a further 20–25 minutes, or until it is cooked through and the skin is golden. When it is ready, remove from the oven and leave to cool to room temperature.

Meanwhile, make the dressing. Mix the tahini with the juice of the lemon, the yoghurt and the extra virgin olive oil. Season to taste.

Trim and finely slice the spring onions, and pick and roughly chop the mint leaves. Toss the mint and spring onions with the rocket and drizzle with a little extra virgin olive oil.

Drizzle the tahini dressing on a serving platter and top with the squash wedges. Scatter with the dressed rocket and dried cherries and finish with a few pinches of sumac.

TOMATO, RUSK AND OLIVE SALAD: *DAKOS SALATA*

Hailing from Crete, dakos is a dish that consists of large barley rusks (paximadi) softened with oil and water and topped with ripe sweet tomatoes. It is then finished with feta or a Cretan cheese called myzithra. This salad is based on that recipe, and is more a meal than a snack or meze. We eat it almost weekly during the summer. Please don't try making it with out of season or unripe tomatoes though; they really do need to be sweet and juicy for this recipe to sing.

SERVES 4–6

½ a red onion
1 tablespoon red wine vinegar
12 black olives
400g ripe tomatoes
6 dakos or wholemeal crispbreads
1 tablespoon capers
2 tablespoons extra virgin olive oil
a few sprigs of basil and
    flat-leaf parsley
sea salt and freshly ground
    black pepper
125g feta
½ teaspoon dried oregano

Peel and finely slice the red onion. Place in a large mixing bowl with the red wine vinegar and leave to one side to soften for 5 minutes.

Remove the stones from the olives and tear into pieces. Chop the tomatoes in a mixture of sizes. Once the red onion has softened, add the tomato and olives to the bowl and crumble in the dakos or crispbreads. Add the capers and extra virgin olive oil. Tear in the basil leaves, roughly chop the parsley and add to the bowl, then season to taste. Crumble over the feta, scatter over the dried oregano and serve.

Recipe overleaf

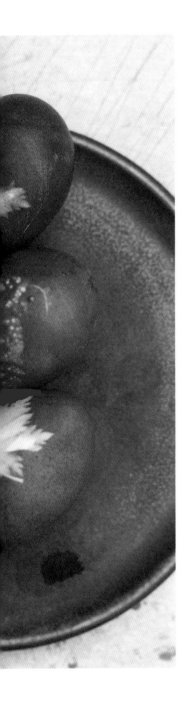

MAMA'S LEFTOVER EASTER EGG SALAD

A creation of my maternal grandmother and mum, this rustic salad is always made after Greek Easter Sunday, when we have an abundance of leftover boiled eggs. Greeks play a game at Easter with dyed boiled eggs (called tsougrisma), where everyone picks an egg and we hit them against each other's to see which break. One egg is always left, and the winner is said to have good luck for the rest of the year. If you listen to my family, however, the egg must be kept for seven years, when it will then turn to gold. I tried this once; I wouldn't recommend it.

SERVES 4–6

400g Cyprus potatoes, or other
   large waxy potatoes
6 large eggs
½ a red onion
3 tablespoons red wine vinegar
250g cooked beetroot
5 ripe tomatoes
1 small Greek or Lebanese cucumber
   (or ½ a regular one)
2 sticks of celery
sea salt and freshly ground
   black pepper
extra virgin olive oil

Bring a large pan of water to the boil. Cook the potatoes whole in their skins, for around 20–25 minutes, or until tender and cooked through. Cook the eggs in the same pan for the last 7 minutes. Remove both and leave to one side to cool.

Peel and finely slice the onion. Place in a large mixing bowl with the red wine vinegar and leave to soften for 5 minutes. Peel the cooked beetroot, if it has the skin on, then chop into 2–3cm chunks and add to the bowl. Chop the tomatoes to a similar size. Peel a few strips off of the cucumber skin and discard, then chop the flesh into small chunks. Trim and finely slice the celery. Add all the prepared veg to the beetroot and onion. Season generously and dress with a couple of tablespoons of extra virgin olive oil.

Flake off and discard the potato skins and cut the potatoes into 3cm chunks. Peel the eggs and slice into wedges. Add both to the salad and set aside for 15 minutes before serving. It won't look like much but this salad is even better after being left overnight in the fridge.

SLOW-COOKED BROAD BEANS AND PEAS IN OIL: *KOUKIA KAI PIZELI LATHERA*

I love this simple side dish. The beans and peas become so sweet and almost sticky in the fresh tomatoes. I've specified fresh veg, for optimum sweetness, but to be honest it is still good using frozen. Just take the time to peel the skins off the broad beans first.

SERVES 6

600g fresh mixed broad beans
  and peas (podded weight)
1 bunch of spring onions
2 garlic cloves
5 tablespoons olive oil
5 ripe tomatoes
sea salt and freshly ground
  black pepper
500ml vegetable stock
1 lemon
½ a bunch of dill or fennel fronds

If any of the broad beans are on the large side, remove the outer skin. Trim and roughly slice the spring onions. Peel and finely chop the garlic.

Place a medium saucepan on a medium-low heat and pour in the olive oil. Sauté the spring onions and garlic for 5 minutes, then add the broad beans and peas. Coarsely grate in the tomatoes, discarding the skin, and season generously. Pour in the stock and bring to the boil, then reduce the heat to low and simmer for 25 minutes, until the veg are tender and the stock has mostly cooked away. Squeeze in the juice of half the lemon. Finely chop and stir in the dill or fennel fronds. Taste and tweak the seasoning, adding more lemon if needed. Stir together well and leave to one side to cool. Serve at room temperature.

CHARRED WHOLE HALLOUMI, NECTARINE AND GLYSTRIDA SALAD

Glystrida is another ingredient I have grown up with but didn't know the english name of until adulthood. In the UK this succulent leaf, that has a very slight tang to it, is called purslane. It is perfect in Greek salads, as we love acidic dressings, picking and using the smallest sweetest leaves possible. If you can't get hold of any, don't despair, this recipe is still wonderful without. You could substitute it with watercress, which despite being a little more peppery would still compliment the salad well.

SERVES 4–6

40g flaked almonds
4 nectarines
1 tablespoon honey
½ a bunch of mint
50g rocket
2 bunches of glystrida (purslane)
2 lemons
extra virgin olive oil
sea salt and freshly ground
   black pepper
250g halloumi

Place the almonds in a dry frying pan and toast over a low heat until golden. Alternatively you can do this in the oven, for 10 minutes at 180°C/gas mark 4.

Put a griddle pan on a high heat. Cut the nectarines into quarters and griddle them on both cut sides, for a couple of minutes so that they are nicely charred. Transfer to a serving plate and drizzle with a little honey. Pick the mint leaves into a bowl with the rocket, and pick in the small leaves of glystrida. Squeeze over the juice of both the lemons and drizzle over a little extra virgin olive oil. Season well and toss together.

Finish by griddling the halloumi whole, for around 3–5 minutes on each side, until nicely charred all over. Transfer to a chopping board and cut into 1cm slices. Transfer the halloumi and scatter over the dressed leaves and toasted almonds. Serve straight away.

ROASTED SAFFRON CAULIFLOWER WITH DATE DRESSING

Growing up, there would always be a packet of dates lying around the kitchen, a healthy(ish) snack that felt, and still feels, like a sweet gift from nature. It wasn't until I was much older, though, that I put two and two together and realised that the gigantic weeping willow-esque tree in my Aunt Frosa's front garden with the little yellow fruits was in fact a fresh date tree – it would produce tonnes of fruit! I still love them dried, in their sticky-toffee state, but I also have a new-found love for them fresh (see page 184). One way I like to use dried dates, as well as in sweet recipes, is in a dressing. They are divine in this simple salad, creating an almost sweet and sour style finish. It's addictive, trust me.

SERVES 4–6

1 large cauliflower, around 1kg
2 onions
a good pinch of saffron
sea salt and freshly ground
  black pepper
1 heaped teaspoon cumin seeds
olive oil
5 medjool dates
2 tablespoons red wine vinegar
1 heaped teaspoon Dijon mustard
4 tablespoons extra virgin olive oil
1 bunch of parsley
1 bunch of mint

Preheat your oven to 200°C/gas mark 6. Trim the cauliflower, discarding only the very outer leaves (leave any younger smaller ones), and cut into even sized florets. Peel and finely slice the onions. Place the saffron in a small bowl, cover with 50ml of boiling water and leave to one side.

Place the cauliflower and onions in a large roasting tray. Season, sprinkle over the cumin seeds and drizzle over the saffron water. Drizzle with olive oil and toss everything together. Pop the tray into the oven and roast for 20–25 minutes, until everything is golden, and the cauliflower is a little crisp and just cooked.

While the cauliflower is roasting, make the date dressing. Remove the stones from the dates, then place them a small mixing bowl and cover with boiling water for 5 minutes. Drain, then place in a blender. Add the red wine vinegar, mustard, extra virgin olive oil and season well. Add a splash of water and blitz everything together until smooth. Pick and roughly chop the parsley and mint leaves.

Spoon the date dressing onto a large serving platter and pile on the roasted cauliflower and onions when they are ready. Top with the chopped herbs and serve.

BRAISED SPICY OKRA WITH OLIVES: *BAMIA LATHERA ME ELIES*

Oh okra, I know I'm not the only person to have a love-hate relationship with this gelatinous vegetable. However it is all about the preparation. If it is chopped, I'm afraid I am not a fan. As soon as the seeds are exposed it become sticky and gloopy. Wonderful for thickening soups and stews but just not my bag I am afraid. If it is cooked whole, braised, roasted or even deep fried, then I am fully on board. The key is to trim the tops in a cone fashion, leaving the body intact, and then toss in a little vinegar or lemon juice.

SERVES 4–6

500g okra
2 tablespoons red wine vinegar
sea salt and freshly ground
    black pepper
2 onions
2 garlic cloves
2 sticks of celery
100ml olive oil
½ teaspoon dried chilli flakes
    (optional)
1 tablespoon tomato purée
5 ripe tomatoes
20 black olives

Prepare the okra by trimming the stalk end. You want to cut it off as if you were sharpening a pencil, so that it is curved with a slight point in the middle, being careful not to expose any of the seeds inside (this is what makes it slimy). Worst case scenario, just trim off the stalks. Toss the okra with the vinegar and a couple of pinches of salt and lay out on a tray to dry out for an hour.

Meanwhile peel and finely slice the onions and garlic. Trim and roughly slice the celery. Pour the olive oil into a large saucepan and place on a medium-low heat. Sauté the sliced veg for 15–20 minutes, until soft and sticky. Stir in ¼ teaspoon of the chilli and the tomato purée. After a minute, coarsely grate in the fresh tomatoes, and tear in the olives, discarding the stones. Bring to the boil, then when the okra is ready stir it in. Season with pepper and cook over a high heat for 3 minutes. Stir everything together well, cover with a lid, then reduce the heat to low and cook for 20–25 minutes, until thickened, rich and cooked through. Taste the sauce, adding a little more chilli if you like and tweak the seasoning. Serve warm.

JEWELLED PILAFI: *POURGOURI ME RODI*

What do Cypriots have as a classic side dish with, well, almost anything? If you go to touristy restaurants on the island you'd be fooled into thinking it is chips or rice. However, if you are being cooked a typical meal in a Cypriot home the accompaniment is mostly salad and pilafi (also called pourgouri, the Greek word for bulgur wheat). It isn't as 'fluffy' as couscous – we cook it to be served a little more moist – not quite a risotto, but somewhere in between.

SERVES 4

2 onions
2 garlic cloves
olive oil
50g vermicelli
1 tablespoon tomato purée
200g coarse bulgur wheat
700ml vegetable stock
sea salt and freshly ground
   black pepper
½ a lemon
1 large bunch of mixed soft herbs,
   a mixture of mint, coriander
   and parsley
a handful of pomegranate seeds
Greek yoghurt, to serve

Peel and finely slice the onions and garlic. Place a medium saucepan on a medium-low heat and drizzle in a couple of tablespoons of olive oil. Fry the onions and garlic for 20 minutes, reducing the heat a little, until golden and caramelised (if needed, add a splash of water along the way). Crush in the vermicelli, add a drizzle more oil, then turn up the heat and fry for a couple of minutes so the pasta becomes toasted and golden. Stir in the tomato purée, then add the bulgur wheat and stock. Bring to the boil, then cover, reduce to a simmer and cook for 10 minutes. Remove from the heat and leave for 10 minutes, covered. Season to taste and stir in the juice of the lemon half, using a fork to fluff it up. Pick the herb leaves, discard the stalks and finely chop them. Stir through the bulgur wheat and serve scattered with the pomegranate seeds and a generous amount of thick Greek yoghurt.

HERBY POTATO SALAD: *PATATOSALATA*

We grew up eating potato salad like this – no mayonnaise in sight. It's so much fresher and more flavoursome, the perfect summery side dish. If you can't find Cyprus potatoes, any waxy potato would work. It would even be glorious with Jersey Royals when they are in season. Don't peel them, though, just wash and flake off the skins. (Photo on page 134.)

SERVES 6–8

1kg Cyprus potatoes or other
   waxy potataoes
1 bunch of spring onions
½ a bunch of coriander
½ a bunch of flat-leaf parsley
2 lemons
extra virgin olive oil
sea salt

Peel the potatoes and cut into 3–4cm chunks. Place in a large pan of water and bring to the boil. Reduce the heat and cook for around 8–10 minutes, or until the potatoes are cooked through. Drain and leave in a colander to steam dry.

While the potatoes are cooking, trim and finely slice the spring onions. Finely chop the coriander and parsley. Place the cooked potatoes in a large mixing bowl and squeeze over the juice of both the lemons, then dress with a few tablespoons of extra virgin olive oil. Season with salt to taste and stir in the spring onions, coriander and parsley.

LEMON ROAST POTATOES WITH ARTICHOKES

I love potatoes cooked this way, and even when artichokes aren't in season I will still cook them like this, with a hefty amount of lemon juice. You can use regular potatoes, such as Maris Pipers; however, if you can, do hunt down Cyprus potatoes – their waxy texture give them a lovely buttery finish.
(Photo on page 164.)

SERVES 6–8

3 lemons
12 artichokes
1.5kg Cyprus potatoes,
   or other waxy potatoes (quartered)
150ml olive oil
sea salt and freshly ground
   black pepper
6 garlic cloves

Halve one of the lemons and squeeze all the juice of both halves into a large bowl of water – you'll need this to prepare the artichokes. Using a serrated knife, trim off the top of the artichokes and a good chunk of the stem. Peel or cut away the tough outer leaves, leaving the tender inner leaves. Trim down the stem to remove the tough skin. Then halve the artichokes and use a teaspoon to scoop out the choke (the fuzzy bit in the middle). Rub the artichokes with the cut lemon halves to stop them browning, then place them in the water.

Preheat the oven to 200°C/gas mark 6. Peel the potatoes and cut into large chunks. Place in a pan of salted water and bring to the boil over a medium heat. Parboil for 5 minutes, then drain and leave in a colander to steam dry.

Drain the artichokes and place them and the potatoes in a roasting tray, then drizzle with the olive oil and season well. Squeeze in the juice from the remaining 2 lemons, crush the garlic cloves with the side of your knife and add these, too, then toss everything together. Spread the veg into one layer, then roast for an hour. Turn the veg over and return to the oven for a further 20 minutes, or until golden and crisp all over.

7

BAKING AND SWEETS

—

CELEBRATION SHORTBREAD: *KOURABIEDES*

I knew I would have a hard time getting this recipe from my Yiayia Martha, as when she bakes kourabiedes she makes around 200 at a time. She makes them at times of celebration – Christmas, Easter, parties – and they'll be made en masse until her dining table and kitchen worktops are piled high with trays to hand out to all her friends and family. They look pretty magical too, enrobed in mountains of dusty icing sugar. And as a result they last well in a sealed container, for days if not weeks.

MAKES 25–30

75g blanched almonds or walnuts
250g unsalted butter, at room
   temperature
500g icing sugar (don't be alarmed –
   you only use 150g in the biscuits)
2 tablespoons brandy
1 large egg yolk
400g plain flour
¼ teaspoon baking powder
a pinch of sea salt
75ml orange blossom water

Preheat the oven to 160°C/gas mark 2–3 and line two baking trays with greaseproof paper.

Place the nuts on one of the trays and toast in the oven for 10 minutes, or until lightly golden. Cube the butter, place in a free-standing mixer and beat until pale and creamy. Sift in 150g of the icing sugar, then add the brandy and egg yolk and continue to mix for a few more minutes.

Finely chop the toasted nuts or blitz in a food processor. Add them to the butter mixture, along with the flour, baking powder and pinch of sea salt, then, using a metal spoon, fold it all together, until combined. Roll spoonfuls of the mixture into balls, then mould each one into a traditional crescent shape. You could also make them into fingers, or cut them with a star cutter – whatever you like.

At this stage I would normally bake them straight away; however, if the mixture feels very soft or if it is a hot day, you could put the shaped biscuits into the fridge for 20 minutes to firm up again. This will stop them spreading too much in the oven.

Place the biscuits on the baking trays and bake for 15–20 minutes, or until lightly golden.

Add a generous amount of the remaining icing sugar to a small, deep tray. Very lightly brush the warm biscuits with orange blossom water and leave to cool slightly for 10 minutes. Place them in the icing sugar tray and toss to coat. Leave in the icing sugar, making sure they are well covered, until serving.

CHRISTMAS HONEY BISCUITS: *MELOMAKARONA*

These are an unusual type of biscuit, in that once they are baked they are drenched in a spiced honey syrup. Despite that, they are not sickly sweet and have been an incredibly popular addition to our kitchen (I seem to have a never-ending supply at the moment). When my Yiayia Martha makes them for us she uses a special ingredient – lager. She swears it makes them a little lighter, so if you want to try her way, substitute the orange juice for something with a little fizz.

MAKES 24

60g unsalted butter, plus extra
    for greasing
175ml light olive oil
100ml fresh orange juice (or lager,
    see introduction)
2 tablespoons brandy
250g caster sugar
600g plain flour
1 teaspoon baking powder
½ teaspoon bicarbonate of soda
½ tablespoon ground cinnamon
1 teaspoon mixed spice
½ teaspoon fine sea salt
150ml honey
1 stick of cinnamon
75g shelled walnuts, almonds
    or pistachios
dried rose petals (optional)

Preheat your oven to 180°C/gas mark 4. Grease two baking sheets with a little butter then line with greaseproof paper.

Melt the butter in a large pan with the oil. Stir in the orange juice (or lager), brandy and 100g of the sugar. Sift in 500g of the flour, the baking powder, bicarbonate of soda, ground cinnamon, mixed spice and salt, then beat it all together until smooth. Add a little more flour if the mixture still feels a little greasy, just enough to bring it all together – it shouldn't be too stiff.

Roll the dough into golf-ball sized pieces, then mould them so they are slightly oval in shape. Place on the greased and lined baking sheets. Bake for around 20–25 minutes, until golden.

Meanwhile make the syrup. Place the honey in a small pan with the remaining 150g of sugar, the stick of cinnamon and 350ml of water and gently bring to the boil over a medium heat. Once it's boiled, turn the heat down to low and leave to simmer for 5–8 minutes, until thickened ever so slightly. Finely chop the nuts ready for the biscuits.

When the biscuits are ready, carefully dip each one into the warm honey syrup, so they are completely coated. Leave them for around 30 seconds on each side, so they soak it up (but not for too long or they'll fall apart). Place the soaked biscuits on a tray and immediately sprinkle them with the chopped nuts and rose petals, if using. Leave to cool before serving.

CARAMELISED FIG SEMOLINA LOAF

I developed this loaf cake using some of my most loved Greek ingredients – figs being one of my favourite fruits of all time. And it is my perfect type of cake – damp, forgiving, delicate. My family loved it so much that my yiayia even asked me for the recipe, which is a really big deal.

SERVES 8–10

230g unsalted butter, at room
   temperature, plus extra for greasing
300g caster sugar
1 orange
3–4 figs (depending on size)
3 large eggs
175g ground almonds
125g semolina
1 heaped teaspoon baking powder
a pinch of fine sea salt
1 tablespoon orange blossom water

Preheat the oven to 180°C/gas mark 4. Grease a 2lb loaf tin and fully line with greaseproof paper.

Cut 30g of butter into cubes and place in a small saucepan on a medium heat to melt. Add 100g of the caster sugar. Finely grate the zest of the orange into a small bowl and keep to one side, then squeeze the juice of half the fruit into the saucepan with the butter. Stir everything together, leave for 4–5 minutes until it has become a light syrup, then pour into the bottom of the lined loaf tin.

Cut the figs into ½cm slices. Line as many of the slices as you can in the bottom of the tin in a single layer, going up the sides a little if possible (don't worry if you have a few slices left).

Cut the remaining 200g of butter into cubes and place in a large bowl with the remaining 200g of caster sugar. Beat with a wooden spoon until pale and creamy – if you have a free-standing mixer, you can make the cake batter easily in there. Beat in the eggs, one at a time, and don't worry if it splits slightly, it will come back together. Add the ground almonds, semolina, baking powder and salt to the bowl and beat everything together till smooth. Stir in the reserved zest and the orange blossom water, and squeeze in the juice from the remaining orange half. Mix together, then pour the batter into the cake tin, over the sliced figs.

Place the cake tin in the middle of the oven for 45–50 minutes, until golden and cooked through. Check it's cooked by inserting a skewer into the middle; it should come out clean with no batter on it. When ready, leave the cake to cool in the tin for 10 minutes, then gently turn it out onto a cooling rack. Peel off the greaseproof and leave to cool almost completely. It's perfect served with a dollop of Greek yoghurt.

ORANGE, YOGHURT AND FILO CAKE: *PORTOKALOPITA*

I don't know how I made it through life without this beauty in it. It's a fairly recent discovery and is everything I want in a cake. It's sticky, citrussy, not too heavy, but unlike anything I have eaten before. It's a cake made of shredded filo and a yoghurt-based custard. Sound intriguing? It is, and if, like me, you're a lover of lemon drizzle cakes, I'm pretty confident that you'll love this too.

SERVES 12

2 oranges
500g filo
400g caster sugar
1 stick of cinnamon
200ml olive oil, plus extra
   for greasing
250g Greek yoghurt
5 large eggs
1 tablespoon baking powder
1 teaspoon vanilla bean paste
   or extract

Place one of the oranges in a small pan and cover with water. Bring to the boil, then reduce the heat to low and simmer for 1 hour. Remove from the heat and leave to cool.

Meanwhile, separate all the sheets of filo and rip them into small pieces around 1–2cm in size, then lay them on a couple of baking sheets or trays so that they dry out. Leave them to one side for 20 minutes.

To make the syrup, place 250g of the sugar in a saucepan with 300ml of water, the stick of cinnamon and the juice of the remaining orange. Place on a medium heat and bring to the boil. Leave to gently bubble away for 10 minutes, until syrupy but not coloured, then remove from the heat and allow to cool completely.

When the filo has dried out, preheat the oven to 180°C/gas mark 4. Grease a 25cm × 30cm cake tin or roasting tray with a little olive oil.

Roughly chop the boiled orange, then place in a food processor or blender and blitz until you have a smooth purée. Spoon half the purée into a small sealable container and freeze for another day. Add the yoghurt to the blender and pulse until incorporated. Spoon into a large mixing bowl and beat in the eggs, the remaining 150g of sugar, olive oil, baking powder and vanilla.

Scatter half the filo into the greased tin and pour in half the yoghurt mixture. Mix it together well, in the tin, so that all the filo is coated. Then repeat with the remaining filo and yoghurt mixture on top (don't worry if it is a little loose, it'll set perfectly). Place in the oven for around 35 minutes, until set and golden.

When the cake is ready, remove from the oven. Pierce lightly with a fork and evenly pour over the cooled syrup and leave for at least 1 hour before slicing and serving, so the syrup has a chance to properly soak in.

PISTACHIO AND STRAWBERRY CELEBRATION CAKE

Strawberries are a quintessential British fruit, but during the summer months you will also find an abundance of strawberry carts all over Cyprus. I have such vivid memories of long drives up the mountains with my grandparents, making frequent stops for punnets of strawberries and cherries, and, of course, stops to light candles and say a prayer at all the religious icons on the way.

Also, I must add, I recently made this as a 3 tier wedding cake, layering it with an orange blossom scented buttercream. The pistachios in the sponge keep it from drying out, which makes it the perfect make-ahead cake. I heard it went down a treat.

SERVES 12–14

225g unsalted butter, plus extra
   for greasing
100g shelled pistachios, plus
   extra to serve
225g caster sugar
200g self-raising flour
½ teaspoon bicarbonate of soda
4 large eggs
1 teaspoon pistachio extract
   (optional)
2 tablespoons milk
200g strawberries
200ml double cream
150g Greek yoghurt
1–2 tablespoons rose water
2 tablespoons icing sugar (optional)

Preheat your oven to 170°C/gas mark 3. Grease and line the base of two 20cm round cake tins.

Blitz the pistachios in a food processor until finely ground. Add the sugar, self-raising flour, bicarbonate of soda, eggs and pistachio extract (if using). Add the butter in cubes and pulse everything together until just mixed. Add the milk and pulse again until you have a smooth batter. Divide between the cake tins and bake for 25–30 minutes, or until golden and cooked through. Leave in the tins for 5 minutes, then transfer to a cooling rack to cool completely.

Hull and slice the strawberries. Whisk the cream to soft peaks and stir in the yoghurt and rose water to taste. When the cakes are cool, sandwich them together with the cream and strawberries and serve sprinkled with any remaining chopped pistachios. Dust with icing sugar, if you like.

TINY SPICED SYRUP DOUGHNUTS: *LOUKOUMADES*

Ah, loukoumades. A sweet that brings together our family from far and wide. These are definitely a treat and not something that is made all the time. They are essentially little doughnuts that are drenched in a spiced sugar syrup. In Greece this syrup is made with honey, but in Cyprus we rarely add honey, using a simple sugar syrup as our base. The dough in each country can be quite different, too, and I prefer the Cypriot one (of course), which often has a cooked potato riced into the batter. This makes them extra crisp on the outside, and fluffy in the middle.

The story behind these is what makes them special. You can buy them all year round, but my family told me they always make them on 6 January, to celebrate Epiphany. Housewives would throw the first ones out of the windows, or leave them on their windowsills, to kill or scare away the kallikantzari (little imps that live underground and come up during the 12 days of Christmas). It's a ritual as important as spring-cleaning the house.

MAKES 45–50

1 potato, around 175g
500g strong bread flour
1 teaspoon fine sea salt
1 × 7g sachet of dried yeast
400g caster sugar
1 stick of cinnamon
3 cloves
½ a lemon
2–3 tablespoons rose water
1 litre vegetable oil
3 tablespoon honey (optional)
toasted sesame seeds (optional)

Peel the potato and cut into even-sized pieces. Place in a small pan of boiling water and simmer for around 10 minutes, until cooked through. Drain and leave to one side to cool.

Place the flour in a large mixing bowl and stir in the salt. In a measuring jug, mix together 625ml of tepid water with the yeast and 1 tablespoon of the sugar. Leave to one side for 5 minutes. Make a well in the flour and pour in the yeast water. Press the cooked potato through a ricer into the mixture, and mix everything with a whisk, beating it and bringing it together. Cover the bowl and leave to one side to prove, for around an hour.

Meanwhile make the syrup. Pour the remaining sugar into a large pan and add 400ml of water. Add the stick of cinnamon, cloves and the juice of the lemon half. Bring to the boil, then simmer for 5–8 minutes, until thickened and syrupy but not too golden. Turn off the heat. Stir in the rose water. I like 3 tablespoons, but if you're not a huge fan just add 2.

When the dough is ready, heat the oil in a medium-sized pan. Place it on a medium heat, and place a piece of bread or potato in there. When the bread starts to sizzle and turns golden, spoon it out – this is when you know your oil is ready. Line a dinner plate with kitchen paper, and place a teaspoon in a mug of water.

The aim is to keep one hand dirty and the other clean. Use one hand
to grab a small amount of the batter, then gently close your hand and
squeeze the batter through your thumb and index finger, almost like a
bubble. Using your clean hand to hold the teaspoon, scoop the bubble
of batter from your hand and carefully drop it into the hot oil. Dip the
teaspoon back into the water and repeat (the water keeps the batter from
sticking to the spoon). Keep going until the pan has a layer of dough balls,
but is not so full that the pan is overcrowded. (You will need to do this in
batches.) Leave them to cook for a few minutes until golden underneath,
then flip them over and cook for a few minutes more.

When cooked through, remove with a slotted spoon, place on the paper-
lined plate to drain off the excess oil, then transfer the balls to the cooled
sugar syrup. Leave the doughnuts in there for a few minutes to soak up
the syrup, then transfer to a platter. Serve straight away, as they are.
Or, for a more Greek-style serving, drizzle with a little honey and scatter
over toasted sesame seeds.

SPICED SESAME BARS: *PASTELLI*

Ask any Greek or Cypriot person what snack reminds them most of all the religious festivals and celebrations (panayiri) and they will say loukoumades (see page 227) and pastelli. Pastelli is a Lenten dish and a great pick-me-up when you need something sweet. I've added some spices, which sing with the honey and make it that little bit more addictive. However, if you want to keep it authentic, leave them out.

MAKES ENOUGH SNACKS FOR A FAMILY FOR 3 DAYS

½ teaspoon coriander seeds
½ teaspoon fennel seeds
¼ teaspoon cumin seeds
100g shelled pistachios
200g sesame seeds
125g caster sugar
8 tablespoons honey

Place a large non-stick frying pan on a medium heat. Toast the coriander, fennel and cumin seeds for a minute, then grind until fine using a pestle and mortar and leave to one side. Line a baking sheet with greaseproof paper.

Roughly chop the pistachios. Toast the sesame seeds and pistachios in the frying pan, tossing occasionally, until golden, then remove from the pan and keep to one side. Stir in the ground spices.

Pour the sugar into the frying pan and leave it to gently melt, but do not stir it or it will crystallise, just swirl it. When all the sugar has melted, carefully pour in the honey and swirl together. Quickly stir in the sesame seed blend. Mix well, then immediately pour/spoon onto the lined baking sheet. Using wet hands, carefully push the mixture out into a thin even layer, around 1cm thick. Leave for 5 minutes, then use a knife to cut the pastelli into bite-sized pieces. It will cool to a hard, yet slightly chewy, moreish snack.

CLASSIC APPLE PIE: *MILOPITA*

This simple, traditional pie was one of the first things I learnt to bake. I remember my mum teaching me, her black and red book open on the counter, filled with recipes passed down by her mum, my Yiayia Maroulla. It isn't difficult, and is one of the most popular pies you'll find in Cyprus – every family has their own version. I've tweaked it ever so slightly, in that I blitz walnuts into the pastry to give it a little more texture.

SERVES 10–12

1kg eating apples
2 large eggs
325g caster sugar
125g walnuts
80ml brandy (or orange juice)
200ml olive oil
400g plain flour
1 teaspoon ground cinnamon
2 teaspoons baking powder
a good pinch of sea salt

Preheat your oven to 180°C/gas mark 4. Peel the apples, cut into quarter wedges, remove the core and then slice widthways as finely as you can, small ½cm slices at the most.

Separate the eggs. In a large clean bowl whisk the egg whites till stiff peaks form (using an electric hand whisk if you have one). Very gently stir in just over half the sugar and the sliced apples.

Place the walnuts in a food processor and pulse until finely chopped (if you don't have a food processor you can do all this by hand or even use ground almonds). Add the egg yolks, brandy, oil, remaining sugar, flour, cinnamon, baking powder and sea salt. Pulse until it all just comes together – it will look like a nutty pastry. If it needs a little more liquid, spoon in the liquid from the bottom of the apple bowl.

Grease a 25cm×30cm tin or tray. Press just over half the pastry mixture onto the base of the tray – using the back of a tablespoon to help you prise it to the edges. Pour the apple and meringue mixture over the top. Then take small balls of the remaining pastry, flatten them out in your hand as thinly as you can, and drape them over the top of the apples. Don't worry if there are little gaps between the pieces of pastry – that is OK. Place in the oven and bake for around 40 minutes, or until golden and cooked through. Leave to cool in the tin, and serve as and when needed.

APRICOT, PINE NUT AND KATAIFI PIE

I adore the method of making tyropita (the cheese pie on page 111) and wanted to play with it and make a sweet version. Although this doesn't have a cheese-based filling, it still works like a dream and is a fantastic celebration of sweet summertime apricots.

SERVES 8

50g unsalted butter
200g kataifi
300g apricots
2 tablespoons apricot jam
4 heaped tablespoons caster sugar
2 eggs
175ml milk
175ml double cream
50g pine nuts
5 tablespoons honey

Grease a 20cm round springform cake tin with the butter. Place two-thirds of the kataifi in the tin and tease it up the sides, letting it drape up over the edge slightly while ensuring the bottom is completely covered.

Stone and finely chop the apricots and mix in a bowl with the jam, sugar and one of the eggs. Spoon into the kataifi-lined tin and fold any overhanging pastry over the top. Top with the remaining pastry. Wrap the base of the cake tin with foil, so it comes up the sides slightly, and place in a baking tray. Whisk together the remaining egg with the milk and cream and pour evenly over the pie, flattening the surface lightly with a fork. Leave to soak in for half an hour.

Meanwhile preheat the oven to 180°C/gas mark 4. After the 30 minutes soaking time is up, scatter the pine nuts over the pie, then pop it into the bottom of the oven and bake for 30 minutes. Remove the pie from the oven, evenly drizzle over the honey and return to the oven for a further 15–20 minutes, or until golden. Leave to cool in the tin for 10 minutes, then slide onto a serving plate, slice and tuck in.

FRANGIPANE BAKLAVA

When I told my family I was developing what I hoped to be an outstanding baklava I was met with mixed reactions. I was messing with a classic, but I don't love the Greek or Cypriot versions, as I often find them too sweet. So I wanted to create something that wasn't tooth-achingly sugary, but was moreish, without diverging too much from traditional recipes. Adding the frangipane layers gives it an added creaminess that you don't often get with baklava, while not feeling too far removed from the original recipe. Thankfully my family approves – it's been given the Socratous seal of approval.

MAKES 30–40 SQUARES

350g caster sugar
125ml honey
1 lemon
3 cloves
250g walnuts
1 teaspoon ground cinnamon
175g almonds and pistachios,
    a mixture
250g unsalted butter, at room
    temperature
1 egg
a pinch of fine sea salt
400g Greek or Middle Eastern filo,
    or 270g supermarket shop-bought

Start by making the syrup. Place 300g of the sugar in a medium saucepan with the honey, the juice of the lemon, the cloves and 300ml of water. Bring to the boil, then simmer for 5 minutes until golden. Turn off the heat and leave to one side to cool completely. This is important – the syrup must be totally cold when it is poured over the hot baklava.

Preheat your oven to 160°C/gas mark 3. Place the walnuts in a food processor with the cinnamon and pulse until ground – you don't want it too fine, but to still have a bit of texture. Spoon it into a bowl. Add the almonds and pistachios to the food processor and pulse until ground, again so they still have a tiny bit of texture. Add 125g of the butter, in chunks, the remaining 50g of caster sugar and the egg. Add a pinch of salt and pulse until you have a thick paste. Melt the remaining 125g of butter.

The number of sheets of filo you have depends on the brand you are using. This is a rough guide as to how many you need, but tweak accordingly. Ultimately you want a large amount on the bottom and top.

Brush a 25cm×30cm roasting tray with butter. Layer with 6–8 sheets of filo if using a thinner type, brushing lightly with butter as you go. If using supermarket bought filo you will only need 3–4 sheets. Spoon over half the chopped walnuts. If using thin filo lay over another 3–4 sheets, if using the slightly thicker filo use just 1–2. Again, lightly brushing with butter as you go. Evenly spoon over half the almond pistachio frangipane mixture. Repeat the layers until the fillings are used up. Finish with a thicker layer of filo, like the base. Using 6–8 sheets of fine filo, or just 3–4 of the thicker type, brushing with the last of the molten butter. Score the top of the baklava with a sharp knife, either in squares or diamonds. I like my baklava quite small, bite sized, so I space the lines around 3–4cm apart.

Place the tray in the oven for 1 hour 15–20 minutes, until golden and crisp. When done, remove from the oven and immediately pour over the cool syrup, as evenly as you can. The baklava will crackle as it absorbs the syrup. Leave to one side to cool completely – if you can bear it, leave for a few hours before tucking in. It's even better the next day.

CUSTARD-FILLED PIES TWO WAYS: YIAYIA MARTHA'S *GALATOBOUREKO* AND A CLASSIC *BOUGATSA*

I have been incredibly lucky to grow up with a constant supply of galatoboureko, as it is one of my Yiayia Martha's specialities – even to this day she makes regularly. We'll often get phone calls exclaiming that there is a tray about to come out the oven and to come and pick it up instantly (there are worse phone calls to get). And I've learnt over the years that, like all regional dishes, there are many ways to make it: in a tray, rolled up like cigars, with and without semolina in the filling… I have kept true to our family recipe and have rolled them into cigars. The shape also means they are criminally easy to eat, and if you make them small they're almost justifiable as finger food, or a light snack. Oh dear.

Alongside our family recipe for galatoboureko, I have included bougatsa, as it is essentially the same ingredients but executed in a slightly different way. Similarly bougatsa can either be made into one big filo pie or individual parcels. Filled with the same custard, it is baked and then finished with icing sugar and cinnamon. Less sweet, and served straight to the table. In my head I see the first as an afternoon tea, and this as dinner-party-worthy.

CREAMY FILLED CIGARS IN AN ORANGE BLOSSOM SYRUP: *GALATOBOUREKO*

MAKES 14

425g caster sugar
4 cloves
1 stick of cinnamon
1 lemon
1 litre milk
125g fine semolina
4 large eggs
100g unsalted butter, plus extra
  for greasing
1 tablespoon orange blossom water
270g filo (for recipe, see page 265)

Start by making the syrup, which needs to be cold when the galatoboureko come out of the oven. Place 300g of the caster sugar in a medium pan with 300ml of water. Add the cloves, stick of cinnamon and peel in the zest of half the lemon. Gently bring the mixture to the boil over a medium heat, then reduce the heat and simmer for 5 minutes until thickened but not coloured. Remove from the heat and leave to one side to cool.

For the custard, start by warming the milk in a large saucepan over a medium-low heat (do not let it boil). In a large mixing bowl, whisk together the remaining 125g of sugar with the semolina and the eggs. Finely grate in the remaining lemon zest. Whisk until pale, then ladle in some of the hot milk and whisk quickly to stop the mixture scrambling. Loosen with a little more of the milk, then pour the egg mixture into the pan. Whisk constantly for 5–10 minutes, until the custard thickens, but be careful not to let it overcook. As soon as it has thickened enough to coat the back of a spoon, remove from the heat, whisk in 40g of the butter and the orange blossom water and leave to cool. Give it a whisk as it cools to stop a skin forming.

When everything is ready, assemble your galatoboureko. Start by pre-heating the oven to 180°C/gas mark 4 and melting the remaining 60g of butter. Lightly butter a 25cm×30cm roasting tray. Take the filo out of the fridge and cut in half widthways. Drape a damp tea towel over the pastry to stop it drying out while you work.

Take your first piece of filo and have one of the shorter edges facing you. Brush with butter. Spoon 2 heaped tablespoons of custard 1cm from the edge, in the middle, then fold the pastry up, rolling the custard slightly. Don't worry if it feels wobbly or oozy, it will come together. Fold in each pastry side towards the centre, then roll the pastry all the way up around the custard, so you have a little cigar. Place in the tin. Repeat with all the sheets of filo and the custard. Brush the tops of the little cigars with the remaining melted butter.

Place the tray in the preheated oven and bake for 35 minutes, or until golden and crisp all around. When done, remove from the oven and immediately pour over the cooled syrup. Set aside to cool completely, giving the custard-filled pastries time to soak up all the syrup.

WARM CUSTARD FILO PIE AND CINNAMON SUGAR: *BOUGATSA*

SERVES 6–8

800ml milk
125g caster sugar
125g fine semolina
4 large eggs
1 orange
100g unsalted butter
200ml double cream
270g filo (for recipe, see page 265)
4 tablespoons icing sugar
1 teaspoon ground cinnamon

Start by making the custard. Pour the milk into a large saucepan and warm over a medium-low heat – it needs to be hot but not boiling. In a large mixing bowl, whisk together the sugar, semolina and eggs. Finely grate in the orange zest. Whisk until pale, then ladle in some of the hot milk and whisk quickly to stop it scrambling. Loosen with a little more of the milk, then pour the egg mixture into the milk pan. Whisk constantly for 5–10 minutes, until the custard thickens, but be careful not to let it overcook. As soon as it has thickened enough to coat the back of a spoon, remove from the heat, whisk in 40g of the butter, the double cream and a squeeze of orange juice. Give it a whisk as it cools to stop a skin forming.

When the custard has thickened and cooled, build the bougatsa. Preheat your oven to 180°C/gas mark 4. Melt the remaining 60g of butter. Brush a 25cm×30cm roasting tray with a little butter and line and layer with most of the filo – keep back a couple of sheets – brushing with the melted butter as you go. You want to line the tray so that there is enough pastry hanging over the sides to fold in later. Spoon the thickened custard into the centre of the filo, top with the final 2 sheets and fold any overhanging pastry over the top to seal. Brush with the last bit of butter. Bake on the bottom of the oven for 35–40 minutes, until golden and crisp all over. Leave to cool for 5 minutes, then dust with the icing sugar and cinnamon and serve while still warm.

QUINCE, BRANDY AND WALNUT TRIFLE: A TWIST ON CHARLOTTA

This decadent, somewhat festive pudding is based on my mum's charlotta, a Cypriot trifle made with sponge, chopped spoon sweets and custard. I've taken it a bit further by adding a couple of extra layers: poached fruit in jelly and a cream layer on top to make it even more of a showstopper. It would make a perfect pudding around Christmas, but shouldn't be reserved only for the festive season. Replace the quince with pears or apples if you can't get hold of them (see cooking instructions below). And adorn it as extravagantly as you wish.

SERVES 12–16

2–3 quince (around 800g),
 or 800g pears
5 cloves
310g caster sugar
3 tablespoons honey
1 lemon
400g plain sponge cake (homemade
 or shop-bought, whatever you like)
75ml brandy
50g spoon sweets, bergamot or
 citrus rind works well (optional)
 (see page 17)
8 gelatine leaves
800ml milk
4 large egg yolks
3 heaped tablespoons cornflour
75g walnuts
sea salt flakes
400ml double cream

Peel the quince and cut into 2cm wedges, cutting out the core. Place in a medium-sized saucepan with the cloves, 150g of the caster sugar, the honey and 750ml water (or just enough to cover). Peel in 2 strips of lemon peel and place on a medium heat. Bring to the boil, then reduce to a simmer and poach for 45 minutes, or until the quince is tender and cooked through. (Keep an eye on the water and top it up occasionally if needed.) If using pears, do exactly the same but poach for 12 minutes, or until just cooked through with a little bite still. Remove the fruit from the syrup and leave to cool completely. Keep the syrup to one side.

Cut the cake into 1½cm slices and line the bottom of a 28cm-diameter serving bowl. Drizzle the cake with the brandy and 3 tablespoons of the fruit poaching syrup. When the fruit is cooled, lay it over the soaked sponge. Finely chop the spoon sweets, if using, and scatter them over the top.

Measure out the poaching syrup, you should have around 500ml left. Top it up with water to make 800ml and pour back into the pan to warm through. Soak the gelatine leaves in a bowl of cold water for 5 minutes, then when they are softened squeeze out the excess water and whisk them into the warmed poaching syrup until totally dissolved. Leave to cool completely, then pour it over the soaked sponge and poached fruit. Cover the dish and refrigerate for at least 4 hours, or until completely set.

When the sponge-jelly layer is set, make the crema (custard) layer. Fill your sink with a few inches of cold water. Heat the milk in a large saucepan over a medium-low heat until warm. Meanwhile, whisk the egg yolks with 60g of caster sugar and the cornflour. Finely grate in the remaining lemon zest. Pour a ladleful of the warmed milk onto the eggs and quickly whisk it in. Repeat with another ladle of milk until the mixture loosens. Pour the egg mixture into the pan of warmed milk and whisk constantly until thickened.

You'll need to be vigilant that it doesn't overcook and scramble. Pour the crema through a sieve into a large mixing bowl and stand this in the cold water in the sink (making sure no water gets into the bowl!) until it has cooled completely. Whisk it as it is cooling down so that a skin doesn't form. When it is completely cool, carefully pour it over the jelly layer. Cover the dish and put it back in the fridge to set.

To make the praline, preheat your oven to 180°C/gas mark 4. Scatter the walnuts on a small baking tray or dish and place in the oven for 8–10 minutes, or until lightly browned. Line a baking tray with greaseproof paper. Pour the remaining 100g of sugar into a large non-stick frying pan and place on a medium heat. Melt the sugar, swirling the pan as it melts, until it is completely molten and a deep caramel colour. Working quickly, scatter in the walnuts, crush in a pinch of salt and pour onto the grease-proof paper. Leave it to set.

When you are ready to serve the trifle, whisk the double cream until you have soft peaks, then spoon it over the set crema. Smash the walnut caramel in a pestle and mortar till you have a mixture of fine and coarse pieces and scatter over the cream (you'll probably have extra, just save it to sprinkle over ice cream for another day). Serve straight away.

LIVANEZIKO, AND A NOD TO *MAHALEPI*

Mahalepi is such a funny pudding. It is so unbelievably simple that there really isn't much point including a recipe here, as it's just cornflour and water cooked together to an almost jelly-like consistency. Once chilled, it is drenched in rose syrup, rose water and sugar, and after a day in the blazing sun it's a refreshing sugar hit. I, and most Cypriots, love it, but I do wonder how much of that is down to nostalgia. There are variations of mahalepi all over the Middle East and livaneziko is what we call the Lebanese version. It is richer, creamier and a little less perfumed, and my absolute favourite. Like a cross between a set custard and a panna cotta. As with mahalepi, it is all about the dressing, as the pudding itself has little flavour, so be generous and brave with your adornment – and try and source mastic if you can (see page 17).

SERVES 8–10

½ teaspoon mastic – it can be made without, so don't worry if you can't get it
250g caster sugar
75g niseste (see page 16) or cornflour
1 litre milk
250ml single cream
30g shelled pistachios, roughly chopped
350ml water
2 tablespoons of orange blossom water

Crush the mastic (if using) with 2 tablespoons of the sugar in a pestle and mortar until you have a powder, and leave to one side.

Mix the niseste or cornflour with enough milk to make a loose paste. Pour the remaining milk into a heavy-based pan and whisk in the cornflour mix. Simmer it over a medium heat and whisk until you have a thick cream consistency. Add the crushed mastic (if using, otherwise add 2 tablespoons of the sugar), whisk well and remove from the heat. Cover the top of the cream with clingfilm to prevent it forming a skin and leave to cool.

Once it has cooled completely, whisk in the cream and pour into a serving dish or dishes, cover, and leave in the fridge to set for at least a couple of hours. When it has set, scatter over the pistachios.

While it's chilling, make the syrup. Place 350ml of water in a small pan with the remaining sugar and gently bring to the boil. Reduce to a simmer and bubble away for 5 minutes until you have a light syrup. Remove from the heat, stir in the orange blossom water, and chill also. Serve large spoonfuls of the set cream, with syrup poured generously over the top. Delicious.

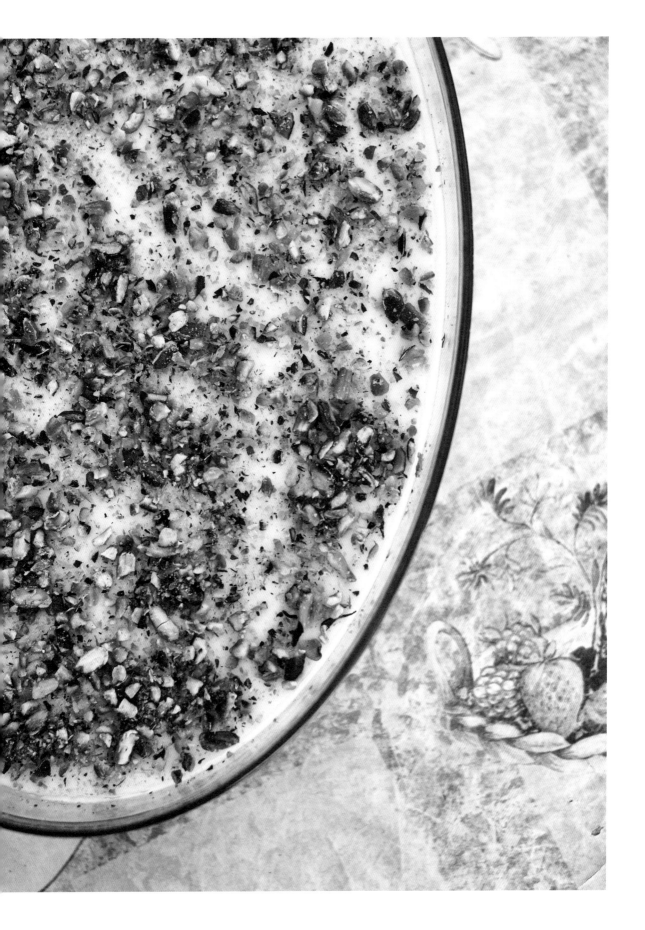

BERGAMOT *LOUKOUMIA*

Loukoumia is what we call Turkish Delight, and it is something found all over Turkey, Greece, Cyprus and the Middle East. As with many traditional recipes you will find bad versions – artificially flavoured, mass-produced versions – and then, in and amongst them, are the gems. Lots of places claim to make the best loukoumia, and I am clearly biased, but a family in my bapou's village of Phini make the best I have ever tried. Ourania inherited the business from her uncle, and their family have made this sweet for a long time. She invited us into her home to show us how it is made, and quite honestly it was a celestial moment. When fresh, loukoumia melts on your tongue. And you needn't worry about the 'Marmite' presence of rose; in the mountains it is flavoured with bergamot, which gives it a much fresher finish.

MAKES... NEVER ENOUGH

neutral/flavourless oil, for greasing
1kg granulated sugar
2–3 bergamots – you will need
    150ml juice
210g cornflour
1 teaspoon cream of tartar
250g icing sugar

You will need a sugar thermometer.

Lightly grease a square cake tin, around 23cm, with a flavourless oil, then line with clingfilm, then grease the clingfilm also.

Place the granulated sugar in a medium saucepan with 500ml of water and 75ml of bergamot juice. Put on a medium heat and stir until the sugar has dissolved. Keep on a high heat for around 15 minutes, until the syrup reaches 115°C on a sugar thermometer – this is called soft ball stage.

In a mixing bowl, whisk together 160g of the cornflour with the cream of tartar. Whisk in 500ml of water until smooth.

Once the syrup has reached 115°C/soft ball stage, whisk in the cornflour mixture. Keep whisking over a medium heat until it becomes thick and gloopy, this will only take a couple of minutes. Turn the heat right down, making sure the pan is on the smallest hob ring you have, and cook for 1½ hours, whisking often, until you have a thick, deep golden mixture. Whisk in the remaining bergamot juice, cook for 5 more minutes, then remove from the heat. Pour the mixture into the greased and lined cake tin and leave to one side for about 4 hours, until it has completely set.

In a large mixing bowl, sift together the remaining 50g of cornflour and the icing sugar. Sift a little straight on top of the loukoumia and then some onto a clean chopping board. Turn the loukoumia block out onto the icing sugar mixture and dust a little more over the top. Carefully cut the block into 2–3cm pieces. Transfer them straight into the bowl of icing sugar and toss them individually, so they are all completely coated. Store in a container, covered with the excess icing sugar mixture, to stop them going sticky (they're far better if not tightly sealed, just covered). Eat within a week.

WATERMELON AND ROSE GRANITA

This recipe is one from my teenage years, when I would visit Cyprus with a gaggle of girlfriends to escape our parents. Back then everything was insanely cheap, and you could pick up a bottle of apple liquor for just a couple of pounds. Not the most refined bottle of booze but at 18 we didn't care. Trying to be a little grown up, we would make trays of watermelon and apple granita to start our nights out. Refreshing and potent. I still make a similar thing, this recipe, but leave out the cheap booze. The most refreshing sweet on a hot summer's day.

SERVES 8

150g caster sugar
1kg watermelon
3 tablespoons rose water
1 lemon

Pour the sugar into a medium-sized saucepan with 300ml water. Give it a stir then place on a medium heat. Bring it to the boil, without stirring, then reduce to a simmer for 5 minutes until the sugar has dissolved but the syrup hasn't coloured. Leave to one side to cool.

Meanwhile remove the skin from the watermelon and cut the flesh into chunks. Blitz with the rose water and juice of the lemon in a blender, in batches if need be. Strain the watermelon through a coarse sieve, pressing it through with a spoon. Mix the sieved watermelon with the cooled sugar syrup and pour into a large deep dish. Place in the freezer for 3–4 hours, then crush the mixture with a fork, creating ice crystals. Return to the freezer for an hour and repeat at least 2 times for fluffy granita. Transfer to a sealable container, and fluff up with a fork before serving

CHERRY, ANISE AND SWEET WINE SORBET

I adore this recipe; it's so intense and punchy that you really don't need a lot of it. Make it either during the summer when sweet black cherries are in season, or any other time with already-prepared frozen cherries. Despite being a summertime sorbet there is something quite festive about the flavour. It would be a wonderful pudding after a rich, wintery dinner, perhaps with a plate of kourabiedes (see page 216).

SERVES 12

250g caster sugar
500g fresh or frozen cherries
  (weight once stones removed)
175ml commandaria or other
  sweet red wine (see page 17)
1 star anise
½ a lemon

Place the sugar, cherries, wine, star anise, juice from the lemon half and 200ml of water into a saucepan. Bring to the boil, then simmer for 5 minutes. Leave to coo slightly. Remove the star anise, then ladle the mixture into a blender and blitz until you have a smooth purée. Place in the fridge to chill, then pour into an ice cream machine and churn according to the machine's instructions. Alternatively, pour into a wide tray and pop into the freezer. Leave to freeze for 3–4 hours, then use a fork to crush the mixture. Return to the freezer and repeat every hour, for around 4 hours, until you have a smooth sorbet. Transfer to a sealable container and freeze until needed. Delicious served with a dollop of softly whipped cream.

RICOTTA, HONEY AND THYME ICE CREAM

This ice cream is astonishingly easy – and elegant at the same time. It shouldn't just be considered for its no-churn method – regardless of whether you have an ice cream machine or not, it is worth making.

SERVES 8

500g ricotta
100g caster sugar
3 bushy sprigs of thyme
400ml double cream
½ a lemon
100ml honey

Blitz the ricotta, caster sugar and picked thyme leaves in a food processor until glossy and combined. Whisk the cream in a large mixing bowl until soft peaks form and then fold in the ricotta mixture. Finely grate in the lemon zest, drizzle in the honey and fold to combine. Spoon into a sealable container. Place in the freezer and freeze for at least 6 hours before serving.

PINK PEPPERCORN, FENNEL AND ROSE ICE CREAM

This delicate and unusual ice cream came about from an ice cream jamming session my friend Holly and I had many moons ago. It was after my Yiayia Martha had brought a big bag of pink peppercorns back from a tree in my bapou's village, and we wanted to find interesting ways to use them. It is a subtle ice cream, and loved by all my family. Think of it as a rose ice cream (triantafyllo) with benefits.

SERVES 8

500ml milk
600ml double cream
2 tablespoons pink peppercorns
1 teaspoon fennel seeds
200g caster sugar
2 teaspoons rose water
3 pieces of rose loukoumia (see page 247) or Turkish delight (optional)

Pour the milk and cream into a large saucepan. Lightly crush the peppercorns and fennel seeds and add to the pan along with the caster sugar. Gently bring to a bare simmer, removing from the heat before the mixture actually starts to bubble. Leave to infuse for 2 hours, then strain, discarding the spices. Stir in the rose water, then refrigerate the cream mixture. When cold, churn in an ice cream machine according to the machine's instructions. Finely chop the loukoumia or Turkish delight, and add to the ice cream for the final 10 minutes of churning. Transfer the ice cream to a lidded container and place in the freezer until needed.

GREEK AND CYPRIOT PITA BREADS

If you've read the section on souvlakia you'll know there are different types of pita. In Greece, kebabs are served wrapped in round, slightly fluffy pita breads. Whereas in Cyprus we use the ones you are more likely to find in shops – the oval ones that open up with a pocket to stuff with meat and salad. The recipe is exactly the same, they're just cooked differently. Both are great, but I still get a thrill when I see the oval ones almost magically puff up in the bottom of the oven.

MAKES 8 PITA BREADS

1 × 7g sachet of yeast
½ tablespoon honey
650g strong bread flour
1 teaspoon fine sea salt
3 tablespoons olive oil

In a large measuring jug, mix 400ml of warm water with the yeast and honey. Leave to one side for 5 minutes. Mix the flour with the salt in a large mixing bowl and make a well in the middle. Pour in the olive oil and the yeast water once it is ready. Whisk the liquids into the flour with a fork until fully incorporated, adding a little more water if the dough feels dry, or a spoonful of flour if it feels too wet.

Turn the dough out onto a lightly floured surface and knead for 10 minutes, until smooth and elastic. Place in a clean bowl, cover with a tea towel and leave to one side to prove for an hour.

For Greek pita bread: place a large frying pan on a medium heat. Knock back the air from the dough and cut the dough into 8 pieces. Place each piece on a lightly oiled worktop and use a rolling pin to carefully and evenly roll the dough into a circle. If you are making them to fill with souvlaki, roll them so they are around 22cm. Pierce each pita around 10 times with a fork. Then cook them one by one in the dry, warm pan for around 2 minutes on each side, until golden and fluffy. Serve straight away, or keep warm in a tea towel until needed.

For Cypriot pita bread: preheat your oven to the highest temperature possible. Place a baking stone or baking sheet at the bottom of the oven. Divide the dough into 8 and use a rolling pin to roll each piece into an oval shape, as thin as you can – around ½cm if possible. Because you need the dough to puff up in the oven, be really careful not to tear or rip the dough, and make sure it is even all the way round. Working as quickly as you can, open the oven door and use a floured spatula to place as many of the pita breads as you can on the heated stone or baking sheet, with the rolled top facing down. Bake the breads for 3–4 minutes, until they start to puff up and turn lightly golden but aren't crisp. Remove from the oven, wrap in a clean tea towel for a few minutes, and serve.

—

SESAME BREAD RINGS: *KOULOURI*

Hands down, koulouri is my favourite bread of all time. There is nothing like a fresh loaf, still slightly warm from the bakers. As rings they are easy to make and look beautiful stacked up as part of a meze or breakfast spread.

MAKES 8–10 RINGS

1 × 7g sachet of dry yeast
60g caster sugar
500g strong bread flour
1 teaspoon fine sea salt
olive oil
150g sesame seeds

In a measuring jug, mix together 300ml of tepid water with the yeast and half the sugar. Set aside for a few minutes. Place the flour in a large mixing bowl and mix in the salt. Make a well in the middle and pour in the yeast water, using a fork to mix it into the flour as you pour. Once it is all mixed together, turn the dough out onto a lightly floured surface and knead it vigorously for 10 minutes, or until it springs back when you poke it (you can of course do this in an electric mixer with a dough hook if you have one).

Lightly grease a large clean mixing bowl with olive oil, then pop in the dough and loosely cover with a clean tea towel. Leave in a warm spot for around an hour, or until it has doubled in size.

Meanwhile, mix the remaining 30g of sugar into 500ml of hot water and pour into a wide shallow bowl (a pasta bowl would be good). Leave to one side to cool completely. Place the sesame seeds in another shallow bowl, or deep-rimmed plate.

Lightly grease two baking sheets with olive oil. When the dough is ready, turn it out onto a lightly floured surface and knock it back. Divide the dough into 8 even pieces. Roll each piece into a thin sausage, and join the ends together to form a ring. Gently lower each ring into the sugar water, then straight into the sesame seeds, making sure each one is completely encrusted.

Pop the rings onto the oiled baking sheet, adjusting the rings if need be to make them into a circle. When they are all done, leave to one side for 20–30 minutes to rise a little. Meanwhile, preheat the oven to 200°C/ gas mark 6.

When the koulouri have finished their second prove, pop them into the oven and bake for about 15–20 minutes, until golden all over. Remove from the oven and leave to cool (or eat warm, I do).

TRADITIONAL CYPRIOT EASTER PASTRIES: *FLAOUNES*

There aren't many recipes in this book that I would label as difficult, or skilled. Cooking, in my opinion, should be accessible, enjoyable and without stress. However, this is one recipe I would say is not for the faint-hearted. It isn't insanely difficult, but boy is it long. There are three components and it needs to be started the day before. If you have tried them and love them, then I urge you to give it a try! Once you've made all the parts, folding the flaounes is actually very relaxing.

As well as being quite an involved recipe, it also requires a little forward planning. You will need to source flaouna cheese, which, as the name suggests, is a cheese made especially for this recipe. It is actually quite bland, but is the perfect texture and vehicle to carry everything else. Check the suppliers on page 298 or hunt down any good Greek, Cypriot or Turkish grocers – they will be able to find it for you.

MAKES AROUND 25

1kg flaouna cheese
500g halloumi
400g mature cheddar
1 large bunch of mint
70g fresh yeast
2 tablespoons caster sugar
16 large eggs
1 teaspoon mastic
1 teaspoon mehlepi
1 teaspoon ground cinnamon
200g raisins
2 tablespoons baking powder
2.5kg strong bread flour
250g sesame seeds
½ a lemon
2 teaspoons fine sea salt
50ml vegetable oil, plus extra
   for greasing
300ml milk

Start the filling the night before. Finely grate the three cheeses, then mix together in a very large bowl and leave to one side to dry out a little. Pick and finely chop the mint leaves, discarding the stalks. In a jug, break up 30g of the yeast and dilute it in 200ml of tepid water with 1 tablespoon of caster sugar. Leave to one side. Whisk together 14 of the eggs.

Grind the mastic and mehlepi, using a small pestle and mortar and a spoon of sugar to stop them sticking. Stir into the grated cheese, along with the ground cinnamon, chopped mint, raisins, baking powder and 650g of the flour, until well combined. Make a well in the middle and pour in the yeast water and two-thirds of the beaten eggs. Use your hands to mix and knead everything together in the bowl, and add more of the beaten egg until you have a slightly damp, doughy mixture. Cover and leave in the fridge (or in a very cool place) overnight.

Place the sesame seeds in a saucepan, cover with plenty of water and squeeze in the juice of the lemon half. Bring to the boil, simmer for 5 minutes, then drain. Cover a tray with a clean tea towel, spread the boiled sesame seeds on it and leave overnight to dry out.

The next day, you are ready to make the flaounes. Start by making the dough. Place 1.6kg of the flour in a large bowl, mix in the salt and make a well in the middle. In a measuring jug, break up the remaining 40g of yeast and dilute with 800ml of tepid water and 1 tablespoon of caster sugar. Pour the vegetable oil into the well in the flour along with the milk and diluted yeast and mix into the flour. Knead together for 10 minutes, turning it out onto a floured surface and adding a splash more water if it is too dry and more flour if it is too wet. You don't want it bone dry, it should still feel a little moist, and the more you knead it, the more it will come together. Grease a large mixing bowl with a little oil, and pop in the dough. Cover with a clean cloth and place in a warm spot to prove for around an hour, or until doubled in size.

Preheat the oven to 220°C/gas mark 7. Whisk the remaining 2 eggs and beat in a tablespoon of the sesame seeds. Use a little of the remaining flour to dust a couple of non-stick baking sheets, and dust a work surface.

Knock back the bread dough. Roll a handful of dough into a large sausage and cut into balls slightly larger than a squash ball. Roll one ball out into a thin circle on a flour-dusted work surface, as thin as you can without tearing it, then press one side of the dough into the dried-out sesame seeds, prodding it in a little so the seeds stick to the underside. Place back on your worktop, sesame side down, and add a large heaped spoonful of the proved cheese dough to the middle of the dough circle, pushing in any raisins or moving them from the top so they don't burn. Fold up the dough edge in four around the cheese filling, leaving a large portion of the filling exposed. Brush with the beaten egg and carefully transfer to a floured baking sheet. Continue until both the trays are full.

Place the flaounes in the oven and bake for 22–28 minutes, until golden all over. Transfer them to a cooling rack, and re-flour the baking sheets. Keep going until both the dough and cheese filling have been used up.

Tuck in while they are still a little warm, or re-warm them in the oven when you want one. We cut them into 2cm slices and eat them with a mug of something warm on the side.

TAHINI CINNAMON SWIRL WITH CAROB: *TAHINOPITA ME CHAROUPI*

These are my absolute Achilles heel when I visit a Cypriot bakery. I cannot resist a fresh tahinopita, and no matter how big it is (and you can get massive ones) I just can't save any for the next day. They are addictive as hell, and were one of the biggest hits with the team when we visited Cyprus for this book.

If you can't get hold of carob syrup don't worry, just leave it out. It'll still work brilliantly and be delicious. To be honest, the addition of carob is a relatively new one to me, you'll mostly find it without. But seeing that one of the areas my family is from is famous for carob (there is a huge old mill in Limassol), I wanted to make a version with it, especially as it adds a rich caramel-like flavour to the filling.

MAKES 4

200g dark tahini
3 tablespoons carob syrup (optional)
125g caster sugar
3 tablespoons olive oil
¼ teaspoon ground cinnamon
fine sea salt
350g bread flour, plus extra
  for dusting
¼ tsp bicarbonate of soda
½ × 7g sachet of yeast
4 tablespoons honey

Preheat the oven to 160°C/gas mark 3.

In a medium mixing bowl, combine the tahini, carob syrup (if using), sugar, 1 tablespoon of olive oil and cinnamon. Add a pinch of salt and leave to one side.

In a large bowl, mix together the flour, bicarbonate of soda and ½ teaspoon of sea salt. Make a well and pour in the remaining olive oil. In a jug, mix together the yeast with 250ml of warm water. Pour into the flour well and mix everything together with a fork. Add a little flour or water as necessary to get the right consistency; you want it to be smooth and elastic, not too sticky or firm.

When the dough is ready, divide into 4 balls. Dust your worktop with flour. Roll one of the balls out into a rough circle to fit the palm of your hand. Hold it and spoon in 1 tablespoon of the tahini mixture. Seal together the dough to encase the tahini and press it flat onto the worktop with the palm of your hand to shape into a rough circle. Spoon in another spoonful of tahini, seal the dough round it, and don't worry if some starts to spill out. This can all be very rough – you just want to build up the dough and tahini layers.

Guide the dough into a long sausage shape, use a knife to spread on a little more tahini mixture, then take each end in each of your hands and twist the sausage in opposite directions so it starts to twirl like a cheese straw. Roll the twirled dough into a spiral, tucking the end underneath, and flatten onto your worktop with the palm of your hand. Place on a lined baking sheet and repeat with the remaining 3 pieces of dough and the tahini mixture.

When they are all ready, bake the tahinopites in the oven for around 20 minutes, until golden and cooked through. Drizzle immediately with honey and leave to absorb for 5 minutes before eating.

HOMEMADE FILO PASTRY

Filo seems to be one of those things that most people refuse to make. If it's a time thing, then I get it, buy ready-made – we've all been there and sometimes life really is too short. But if it is a skill thing, then honestly it is so easy – it really doesn't take much skill at all, I swear. Just patience. And as with all these things, it genuinely does taste better homemade. Unless you are making baklava, then I would definitely use the shop-bought extra fine stuff.

You can use red or white wine vinegar, whichever you have.

MAKES ABOUT 300G

250g plain flour
50ml olive oil
½ teaspoon fine sea salt
½ tablespoon wine vinegar

Lightly flour a clean worktop. Place the flour in a large mixing bowl and pour in the oil and salt. Rub the oil into the flour to create fine crumbs, then add the vinegar and 100ml of water. Mix it all together. If the dough feels a little dry, add a further tablespoon of water. Turn out onto the floured surface and knead until smooth. This should take around 5–10 minutes. Wrap the dough in clingfilm and leave to rest for 1 hour, so it's easier to roll.

When it comes to rolling out the pastry you have two options: by hand or in a pasta machine. If rolling out by hand, cut off a small ball of dough and flatten it on a lightly floured surface. Start rolling away from you, and keep doing this, turning the dough after each roll at 90 degrees in one direction, so you end up with an even circle. Keep going until you have a very thin pastry.

Alternatively, roll pieces of the dough through a pasta machine, starting with the thickest setting and working your way down to the thinnest. And don't worry if the sheets tear in places, no one will notice when you've wrapped your heavenly spanakopita. They'll just be impressed you made your own filo.

Use the filo however you wish – just be sure to keep it wrapped up well before use, to stop it drying out.

8

DRINKS

—

HOMEMADE ROSE SYRUP: *TRIANTAFYLLO*

On my first big trip on my own to Cyprus I became obsessed with the idea of making rose syrup and rose water. Our house in the mountains is surrounded by the most fragrant and full roses, and I spent hours picking and cleaning them. Rose water, as I soon realised, wasn't doable in a domestic kitchen; however, rose syrup I could make (shame I didn't figure this out sooner; I was young though, and eager). I appreciate it is an acquired taste and not everyone's cup of tea. However, used respectfully it is bliss. Not just for desserts, we also use it as a cordial, topped with either water or milk and lots of ice.

MAKES 750ML

500g caster sugar
1 lemon
4 tablespoons rose water
a drop of natural red food colouring
   (optional)

Pour the sugar into a large saucepan with 400ml of water and place on a medium heat. Stir until the sugar has dissolved, then leave to gently cook for 5 minutes until thickened, but before it has a chance to turn golden – you want a light syrup, not a caramel. Squeeze in the lemon juice, then add enough rose water to get the desired strength – I add around 4 tablespoons. Add a drop of food colouring, if you like. Shop-bought triantafyllo is always bright pink in colour, and is pretty when finishing puddings.

—

AUNTIE FROSA'S LEMON (OR MANDARIN) CORDIAL: *LEMONADA*

I've attributed this recipe to my Aunt Frosa, whom I adore, as she always has a bottle of homemade cordial in her fridge. But to be honest it could be almost any Cypriot household's recipe, it is so simple and made everywhere. During the winter months, when there is an abundance of citrus fruits on the island, this was and is another way of preserving them. Here I have given you the ratio for lemons – lemonada – however, it can easily be made with mandarins, oranges or any citrus fruit you have to hand. Just tweak the sugar accordingly: if your fruit is a little sweeter, start with less and work from there.

MAKES AROUND 1 LITRE

500ml lemon juice (around
   15 lemons)
450g caster sugar

Start by sterilising a 1 litre glass bottle – the easiest way is to thoroughly wash it, then place it for 10 minutes, in the oven on a very low heat.

Meanwhile squeeze the juice from the lemons into a large saucepan. Stir in the sugar until mostly dissolved and place on a low heat. Warm through for 3–4 minutes, just until the sugar has completely dissolved and the cordial has warmed through; you don't want to bring it to the boil at all. Pour straight into the sterilised bottle and seal. Keeps for up to a year, and once opened store in the fridge. Serve topped with cold water and lots of ice.

SWEET ALMOND MILK: *SOUMADA*

I adore spring time in Cyprus. There is probably more going on in terms of produce around the summer and autumn months, but the landscape in the spring is breathtaking and the almond trees are one of my favourite sights. There are villages in and around the mountains that celebrate the almond tree blossom in February, with festivals and mounds of almond-based treats.

Long before I even knew what trendy almond milk was, there was always a bottle of soumada around. Especially at my Yiayia Maroulla's house – she loved a mug of it before bed (although that could also explain why she was never able to sleep, bless her. It is quite sweet!).

MAKES AROUND 2 LITRES

a handful of bitter almonds
    (or a couple of drops of
    almond extract)
500g blanched almonds
500g caster sugar
1 small stick of cinnamon

If you have bitter almonds, place in a saucepan and cover with water. Bring to the boil on a high heat, and simmer for 2 minutes. Drain and run under cold water, rubbing the skins off as you do. Place them in a food processor with the blanched almonds and pulse until roughly chopped. Add 2 tablespoons of sugar and blitz until finely ground.

Pour 1.75 litres of water into a large saucepan and add the cinnamon stick and remaining sugar. Bring to the boil over a medium heat, then simmer for 5 minutes. Stir in the ground almonds and continue to simmer for 10 more minutes. If using almond extract, add a couple of drops now, but not too much or it'll overpower the drink. Remove the cinnamon stick from the pan and leave to one side to cool completely. After 2 hours, use a muslin-lined sieve to strain the soumada into a clean large pan. Store in sterilised bottles or jars, in a dark place or the fridge until needed. Serve by spooning 2–3 tablespoons into a glass or mug and topping with either cold or hot water.

MOUNTAIN TEAS

Because of where Cyprus is positioned geographically and its consistent climate, you will find hundreds of types of herbs grown there. As a result, for centuries herbs have been used not only for flavouring food and drink, but more as medicinal remedies and infusions (Cyprus was also famous for herb trading). There are few ailments that cannot be relieved by herbs. Here are just a few of the teas that a yiayia might recommend if you are in need.

Mint: digestion

Glykaniso (aniseed): IBS, period pains and constipation in babies (carob is also good for this).

Elderflower: a cooled infusion is used on tired and puffy eyes but it is also drunk to soothe sore throats and colds

Chamomile: insomnia

Fennel seeds: good for breastfeeding mums

Olive leaves: osteoporosis, blood pressure, diabetes

Sage: sore throats and colds, especially when mixed with honey

Ironwort: rich in iron

Savory: reflux

Pomegranate blossom: stops diarrhoea

Cherry stalks: help the kidneys, a diuretic

Calendula: bladder infections

CYPRIOT TEA: *TSAI/CHAI*

Long before I had heard of Indian masala chai, chai to me meant 'Cypriot tea'. The tea we made in the afternoon, if relatives were visiting or if we just felt like it. When a pot was warmed, a few bags of regular breakfast tea were brewed along with a stick of cinnamon and a few cloves. Lightly spiced and always finished with a touch of sugar or honey, it is such a comforting drink and a simple way of enhancing an already much loved beverage.

GREEK COFFEE, TWO WAYS

Greeks and Cypriots take their coffee very seriously. One of my earliest memories was shaking our frappe shaker, which looked a bit like a plastic brown cocktail shaker, whilst walking around our apartment in Limassol. I was only young, but even then I knew the importance of coffee.

So, coffee two ways – the first, hot, small and strong, and the second cold, long and mostly sweet.

The ritual of making Greek coffee is terribly important. It is one of the only things I haven't seen pimped or changed over the years. Always made in a briki (or, as we Cypriots colloquially call it, a gesve, which is based on the Turkish word for the same utensil), most Greek households will have a few of various sizes. It is a long-handled, small, high-sided saucepan, just big enough to make coffee. It also uses a specific type of coffee that is very fine – it isn't filtered out, and cannot be rushed. God forbid your coffee doesn't form kaimaki (the creamy layer) on top.

Iced coffee, or frappe, is found all over Greece and Cyprus, and is probably the most popular drink. Unlike hot Greek coffee there are all sorts of gadgets now to make the best frappe, however this is the traditional way. Shaken, also with a good crema on top.

ELLINIKO KAFE OR KYPRIAKO KAFE

SERVES 1

1 heaped teaspoon Greek coffee

sugar

The first question when you order, or are making, Greek coffee is 'would you like it sketo (plain – no sugar), metrio (medium – 1 sugar) or glyki (sweet – 2 sugars). Establish this and you are good to go.

Fill the coffee cup with water and pour into a briki – Greek coffee cups are small, just a little bigger than an espresso cup. Into the briki stir the coffee and the desired amount of sugar. Place the briki on a medium heat and stir well for a minute to dissolve the sugar. Don't stir it again and leave it to gently come to the boil, but do not let it actually bubble over. As soon as it is bubbling around the sides and rises, remove from the heat and gently pour into your cup. Serve with a glass of ice-cold water on the side, and leave for a few minutes before drinking so the coffee settles to the bottom of the cup. Drink slowly, and when you are done find an old lady to read your fortune from the remaining coffee sediment.

FRAPPE

SERVES 1

1 heaped teaspoon of Nescafé
   (or other dried coffee granules)
large handful of ice cubes
sugar, to taste
splash of full fat milk

Place the Nescafé in a cocktail shaker with the ice cubes, sugar – if using (I like 1 teaspoon in frappe), and 200ml of cold water. Shake vigorously for a minute and then pour into a long glass. You should have a creamy-looking iced coffee. Top with the milk, or if you want it to stay black, just more ice-cold water.

THE PERSEPHONE

This pretty party drink was a happy accident. When we came to the end of shooting this book I wanted to celebrate with the amazing team behind it and popped a few bottles of prosecco in the fridge for the end of the shoot day. In an attempt to jazz it up I added a splash of homemade rose syrup to each glass and a scattering of pomegranate seeds. Not only is it a delight to look at but it tastes heavenly too, and has become a firm favourite in our house. I've attributed the recipe to my daughter Persephone, due to the pomegranate seeds in there, not because of her love of prosecco (she has only just turned one). The story of Persephone and the pomegranate is full of hope and the promise of new life, and is why we chose such a big name for our little girl. As a result you will find pomegranate paraphernalia everywhere in our house.

PER SERVING

1–2 tablespoons homemade rose
   syrup (see page 270)
150ml prosecco
a few pomegranate seeds

Pour the rose syrup into the glass and top with the prosecco – the amount of syrup will depend on your personal taste. I love 2 tablespoons, but make a test glass first and see what works for you. Finish with a scattering of pomegranate seeds and serve.

MASTIHA AND BASIL SMASH

We drank something similar to this long cocktail whilst travelling around the Greek islands, and it has been firmly logged in my brain ever since. I absolutely adore it, and think of it as Greece's version of a mojito. It does involve buying a bottle of mastiha (or mastic) liqueur; however, it is readily available now in the UK (see page 298 for suppliers' details). Perfect for a summertime garden gathering.

SERVES 1

50ml mastiha liqueur
1 tablespoon of sugar syrup or honey
¼ lemon
a couple of sprigs of basil
handful of ice
soda water

Place the mastiha liqueur in a cocktail shaker with the sugar syrup. Squeeze in the lemon juice and pick in the basil leaves. Put the stalks in too, and add the ice. Shake everything together vigorously for a minute, and then pour straight into a large glass. Pick out the basil stalks and top with soda water. Serve straight away.

RAKOMELO

My cousin Cassie introduced this drink to me, describing it as Greece's answer to mulled wine. Originally a Cretan drink, rakomelo is now found all over Greece and with good reason – it is delicious! I treat it like a hot toddy and particularly like it medicinally if my throat is feeling a little sore.

SERVES 2

100ml tsipouro/raki
5 tablespoons honey
¼ teaspoon ground cinnamon
2 cloves

Place all the ingredients in a small saucepan and slowly warm through, until the honey has dissolved and the tsipouro or raki is hot but not boiling. Serve, discarding the cloves.

BRANDY SOUR

If Cyprus had to be summed up in a cocktail, this would be it. Served everywhere you go, it uses two of the country's favourite ingredients – brandy and lemon. It was apparently created in the 1930s for an Egyptian king who loved to holiday on the island (specifically Platres in the Troodos mountains – one of my favourite places). Rumour has it that he wanted to disguise his love of alcoholic cocktails, so they created something that looked like iced tea – the brandy sour. This is the traditional recipe, using lemon cordial, which is freshly made everywhere you go.

SERVES 1

ice cubes
a few drops of angostura bitters
60ml brandy (Cypriot if possible)
30ml lemon cordial (see page 271)
   or 20ml of fresh lemon juice
   and 10ml of sugar syrup
lemonade or soda

Fill a long glass with ice and add the angostura bitters. Stir in the brandy and cordial, mix together well, then top with lemonade or soda, depending on how sweet you like your drinks.

Index

SUPPLIERS

Almost every ingredient in this book should be easy to source; however, there may be a couple of harder-to-come-by ingredients that are easily ordered online (where possible, I have given alternatives and options to use without). Those of you that want to go the whole hog, though, check out the companies below.

Despinas – one of the best Cypriot shops I know. Well stocked, they always import the best seasonal Cypriot and Greek produce. They do home delivery all over the UK, but if you can visit you'll be glad you did, as they make the best koupes in town.
http://www.despinafoods.co.uk/

Kupros Dairy – using a family inherited recipe, these guys make the best halloumi and feta outside of Cyprus.
https://kupros.london/

Rooted Spices – fragrant, well-sourced spices. Interesting blends, or straight up, you can find ingredients such as pul biber or mehlebi/mahleb.
https://rootedspices.com/

The Vinegar Shed – not just a home for artisan vinegars, but also a great stockist of interesting herbs and spices, including wild Greek herbs.
https://www.vinegarshed.com/

Cypressa
http://www.cypressa.co.uk/

Odysea
http://www.odysea.com/

Cyprus BBQ
https://www.cyprusbbq.co.uk/

Sous Chef
https://www.souschef.co.uk/

Thank Yous

My grandparents.
This book is for
all of you, for
your courage
and hard work.

—

Bapou Eftihi, you continue to be an inspiration to me, I've never known a person to work so hard, whilst being such a gentle soul. The way you always cried at Jerry Springer, not quite getting the tongue-in-cheek nature, will forever make me smile. Yiayia Maroulla, I'll never be able to articulate how much I miss you. Your laugh, how you'd always be peeling fruit at any given moment, your daily walks to find the most fragrant coriander or spinach leaves. Your strength and stoic ways. You never moaned. I am so grateful to have had you both in my life for so long.

Bapou Taki, some of my happiest childhood memories were bouncing around on your shoulders, whilst walking around the restaurant. The cigars, your endless collection of kitchen knives, the cameras I keep inheriting. I love your collections and appreciation for beautiful things. Yiayia Martha, there is no doubt in my mind that I have inherited your feeding ways, your affinity with baking, instinctive cooking style and love of craft. So much I have learnt in the kitchen is from and because of you. Thank you for always calling me up when you have a recipe to share, something new to try, and forever being my mentor.

Mum, thank you for always encouraging me, for your patience and for teaching me everything you know. For baking cakes with me when I was barely out of nappies and for always feeding us home-cooked food. Dad, thank you for being my guinea pig, and for all the honest feedback! Occasionally you get it right. Lulu, your support and cheerleading is unrivalled. Thank you for making our days playing at the restaurant so much more fun.

Lala, you are the best project manager I will ever meet. Thank you for sorting and arranging our Cyprus shoot, this book is infinitely more beautiful because of your input. Cassie, for always being my food partner in crime, and for sharing all your knowledge and stories of Greece. And being my soundboard.

All my aunts and uncles, in particular Frosa, George, Vasso, Andri, Haroulla, Antonitsa, Katia, Anrico, Androulla, Dolly, Spiroulla, Yiota, Antoni, Elpiniki,

Socrates, Lenia – for teaching me, taking me under your wings and sharing your stories and recipes with me.

Rowan, for believing in me and helping my dream come true, and knowing how important it is to me. Kristin, I have loved working with you so much. Your vision, your style – thank you for coming to Cyprus and embracing my family. You are one of us now. Tab, there are no words to express how grateful I am that you chose to spend precious days shooting with us, for saving plastic tablecloths from Greek bins a year before we even started shooting. Anna, thank you for your stunning design, for creating such a calm, yet embracing book. And for really listening to all my thoughts and ideas. Isla, for your loyalty and going above and beyond. Holly, where do I even begin! For the shoot days, testing, editing, advice and friendship. And for always being honest. I trust you with everything. Sam, I know you work hard, but thank you for being Persephone's new best mate and for the addictive, endless iced coffees! Annie, thank you for working so tirelessly on the book and for your dedication. I appreciate it no end.

Carl, Heather and Claire, thank you for all your support and for bending over backwards to look after Persephone so I could be a working mama. I don't know how I would have done it all without you.

Jamie, thank you for being a brilliant boss for so many years, your advice and kind words. Let me know when you're ready to move to Ithaka. Olia, my Cypriot soul sister, your support means a lot from someone who knows Cyprus as well as you do. Tessa, I feel proud to have the approval of a writer who has influenced my cooking so much.

Thank you to all the following people for your help, recipes, testing time, belief, love and support: India, Sarah, Ewan, Laura Goodman, Andy, Alex, Elly (I'll always be indebted to you), Heather, Felicity, Lucy, Myles, Kayleigh, Adam, Clara, Laura and Ari. To Chloe and Sapphire for your hard work and helping spread the love.

And finally my brood. Pete, I couldn't have done any of this without you. I know it has been tough, a sleep-deprived juggling act like no other, and I can't thank you enough for always having my back and pushing me. And Archie and Persephone. For being my drive to keep these memories alive, and our recipes shared. I love you all. x

ABOUT THE AUTHOR

Georgina is a food writer and stylist from North London.

Growing up above her grandparents' Greek Cypriot taverna in Tufnell Park, she developed a love of cooking from the recipes passed down to her. As a teenager she ran a stall at a farmers' market and worked in restaurants, before studying Fine Art at university. Her passion for food landed her a job as a food writer and stylist on various food magazines, until she joined Jamie Oliver's food team where she worked for twelve years. She now writes, develops and styles for magazines, books, television and campaigns. She also writes an online family food blog: georginahayden.com.

Georgina's work is inspired by her family, her heritage and her love of travel. There is nothing she treasures more than cooking with her mum and her yiayia (grandmother). She documents her food adventures on her two instagram accounts @georgiepuddingnpie and @peaandthepod. Her first book, *Stirring Slowly*, was published in 2016, and *Taverna* is her second.

10

Square Peg, an imprint of Vintage, is part of the
Penguin Random House group of companies
Vintage, Penguin Random House UK, One Embassy Gardens,
8 Viaduct Gardens, London SW11 7BW

penguin.co.uk/vintage
global.penguinrandomhouse.com

The authorised representative in the EEA is Penguin Random House Ireland, Morrison Chambers, 32
Nassau Street, Dublin D02 YH68

A CIP catalogue record for this book is available from the British Library

ISBN 9780224101646

Design by Anna Green at Siulen Design
Illustrations by Kristiina Haapalainen & Sami Vähä-Aho at Polka Paper
Photography by Kristin Perers
Food styling by Georgina Hayden
Props by Tabitha Hawkins

Printed and bound by C & C Offset Printing Co., Ltd

Penguin Random House is committed to a sustainable future for our business,
our readers and our planet. This book is made from Forest Stewardship Council® certified paper.